*Rarely does one find a book with such emotional impact that it forever changes the way the reader views his situation in life. Writing from the keen insight of one who's "been there and done that." Frank Keefer strips away the excuses that we all use as reasons for our lack of success.*

# Reflections of a Master

**Reflections of a Master** is a study of cause and effect. It is a primer for personal accountability.

As you journey through the pages of this book, you will alternatively be grabbed by the throat and shaken up or mesmerized into a state of contemplation. Either way you will be forced to take stock of your own station in life. You will begin to recognize that you are a result of the choices you have made.

The author unapologetically drives home that although your life may be affected by your experience, sometimes outside of your control, the real determining factor of where you are, is the choices that you have made relative to those experiences.

**Reflections** is about basic leadership - accepting responsibility for your own actions. It is a wake up call for those wishing to move beyond where they are.

If you have the courage to read this book, it will change your life.

"*Reflections of a Master* is just what the title says it is. Frank Keefer is the *Real Deal*—and in a world of pretenders and imposters, he's a *Rare Deal*, as well. *Reflections* is a book about LEADERSHIP and Frank Keefer is an INSPIRATION."

—**John Milton Fogg**
**Author,** *The Greatest*
*Networker in the World*
www.greatestnetworker.com

"**WOW**!!! The title of this book is so apropos. Frank is a man who knows where he is going and **EXACTLY** how to get there. He leads by example and judges by results. Anyone who picks up this Masterpiece will be blessed!!! It will be a best seller."

--**Ruby Miller Lyman**
**Network Marketing Pioneer**

"Character is what distinguishes a **MASTER** from someone who is simply technically proficient. Frank is a **MASTER**, not only in network marketing, but also in life. If you are looking to build people for long-term success. This is the MANUAL. It has the principles, speaks to the heart and stirs one to action. This is a must read!"

--**Brian Klemmer**
**Founder, Personal Mastery**
**Seminars. Author,** *If How*
*To's Were Enough, We would*
*All Be Skinny, Rich and Happy*

"I highly recommend reading **Reflections of a Master**. I couldn't put it down! I read it to the end, then opened it back to page 1 and started again. Every chapter is worth reading several times. Written in a simple format where you won't forget the message. Great book, highly inspirational."

-**Tim Sales**
**Creator of** *Brilliant Compensation*

"I just finished **_Reflections_** and must tell you there's an enormous lump in my throat. I loved it...absolutely loved it! Frank truly IS the best in the industry, a Real Warrior for the best our industry has to offer. **_Reflections of a Master_** should be thrown down as a gauntlet to challenge the minds and hearts of everyone (new distributors and prospects alike)...I can hardly wait for the next leg of the journey."

**-Cindy Samuelson**
**New Vision**

"Reflections is not another 'How to...' It lays out the solutions that everyone is crying for whether they are in network marketing or not. It demonstrates the humor of values. Each chapter sneaks up and kicks you in the stomach! It's not preachy and it doesn't dictate, but it does empower! This is a book I can honestly recommend to my field sales force. This book will change the lives of many people."

**-Kathleen Deoul**
**Nikken, Inc.**

"Frank is one of the best network marketers in the industry. He is a Master Instructor and teaches in a way that is exciting and fun. His stories and how they relate to the industry will inspire and motivate you. Sit back, enjoy and learn. This is definitely a must read!!!"

**-Elizabeth Weber**
**International Field President**
**Market America**

# Reflections
## of a
## Master

*Best wishes,*

*Frank J. Keefer*

Frank J. Keefer

# Reflections of a Master

ISBN: 0-9702667-2-3
LCCN:

Copyright © 2001 by Frank J. Keefer
Published by Proteus Press
300 Puppy Smith, Suite 205-290, Aspen, CO 81611
tel. 970-927-9380 fax 970-927-0112

# Table of Contents

Dedication
Acknowledgements
Forward: *by John Milton Fogg*
Preface:
Introduction: *A Journey to Success.*

**Reflections on:**

# *Dedication*

*This book is dedicated to the gals who shaped my life:*

*To my Mom, Anna-rae Heil,*
*Your resilience is truly inspiring. I love you more than words*
*can express.*

*To Gingie, my bride and the love of my life.*
*Your radiant smile and goodness light up my life.*

*To my daughter Lucy,*
*For being My Princess and for the Privacy Club.*

*To my Mother-in-law, Ginny Freeman.*
*God broke the mold when he created you. You're the best!*

*And to my Grandmothers, Lottie Keefer and Bessie Rupp*
*You'll live in my heart forever!*

# Acknowledgements

To Mark Magliocco who introduced me to this wonderful industry over a dozen years ago. Sadly, he left the industry shortly thereafter. No doubt he would be a very wealthy man today had he stayed. Through me, the seed that he planted has grown to positively change the lives of tens of thousands of people, perhaps even hundreds of thousands.

Next, my mentor, Nathan Ricks. Young enough to be my son, Nate, next to my Step Dad, is the hardest working man that I have ever known. When we first met, he was still sleeping in cars and on sofas as he journeyed the country spreading the word of his opportunity. Outside of his company, he is one of the unsung heroes of the industry.

Also, Scott and Nancy Tillotsin who invited me and Gingie into their home whenever we were in Utah. They made us part of their family. It was a wonderful feeling that we will always remember.

Richard Kall's heartfelt stories about the love that he has for his family and how this industry facilitated the expression of that love, pushed my hot button over a decade ago and changed my life forever.

Tony and Pam Bowling, whose never ending patience taught me my left from my right and to count to two. They are two of the most wonderful people that God ever put on this planet.

Elizabeth Weber who shared with me the secret of getting people to events and who, with her husband Bruce, proved that money doesn't change people, it only accentuates who they really are.

My mentors, Dale Solarz, for keeping me straight; Lou Manfredi, just for being Lou, and his wife Charlotte; Randy and Tracy Wojta, who believed in me; the First Lady of Network Marketing, Arlene Lowy, "my second wife," who has been encouraging me for years to lay pen to paper. Her compassion for people is incalculable; Andy Webb who has fulfilled his dream of lifting weights and playing with his kids and to his Mom, Snooks, who is working to increase his inheritance.Also to Mark Zuckerbrod who was always there. I wouldn't be where I am without you guys. Words can't express my gratitude.

To my friend, the ever dynamic *Mr. Attitude*, and his lovely wife, Keith and Kim Doyle and to Ben Ginder, the *Best Dressed Gentleman* in the industry.

To Ed Heil, Sr, a tough, old marine, for his indomitable spirit, for coming into my family and for his love of my mother and the rest of the family.

To my son, Frank III, whose intellect and compassion gives him the capacity to far exceed my success in this, or any, business and for being the type of person that I would want to associate with even if he weren't my son.

Susan Anderson, Tony & Donna Patti, Fran Dobinski and Maria Milad for keeping the ember burning and the dream alive.

The Fitzgeralds, Bobbie, Theresa, Sheila and Carole for inviting me into their family.

My good friends Dani Canubas, Dr. Ed Delos Reyes and Dr. Keith Fisher. Also Dale Dixon, Tony Genova and Captain Jimmy Hohne.

Joe Nawrozki, James Webb and Roger Carlsen for encouraging me to venture into the literary world.

Malcolm Patterson and Chip Emely for their technical support.

To Dick & Moe Grimes and Jon Machmuller for their friendship.

Jim and Loren Ridinger for "the Plan" and for succeeding so that others could achieve their dreams. To *Mr. Energy*, Dennis Franks, for his candor and loyalty to the mission and to his lovely wife, Nancy; to Uncle Marty and Jerry & Isabelle. Also, Kevin Buckman, who used to run a Nuclear Power Plant.

For their support, Marc Ashley, Joe Bolyard, Paul Johnson, Ric Williams, Donna Bowman, Hedy Breckenridge, Andrew Weissman and Anthony Akers. Also Dave Randall, Christy Myers and Carol McLennan

The pioneers, Dave & Maria Silva, Earl & Shirley Seall, Marge & Mickey Hurly, Rick Hannon, Mark & Julie Scholl, Bobby Cannata and Steve Seigh.

Phil & Sue Quido, Bill & Ellie Haldeman, Nina Hale, Steve Harris, Jeanette & Ernie Heikes, Caroline Huang, Ming Chu Kuo, Bonnie & Scott Philo, Sam Pitts, Norm Roth, Jeff & Cristie Schneider, T.A. Taylor Hunt & Rob Grant, David & Stacey Whited and Roger Wu.

Marda Arkebauer, Charley & Peggy Baer, Carole Brubaker, Paul & Lisa Carlotta, Marilyn Freese, Dan & Dawndee Gaub, Mary Susan Haaf, Larry Headings, Mel Hurst, Dan & Deb Sjoberg, Doug & Diana Smith, Mary Strong, Jim & Linda Winkler, Paul & Teresa Carney, Lisa & Edward Grant, Lana & Ken Obrist, Roy Gingrich, Terry Hake, Denis & Connie Hamm, Fred Kerstetter, Sam & Mary Livingston, Deb Moser, Rachel & Shane Patterson, George & Judy Reichley, Mike & Yolanda Schiavone, Alan & Debbie Yentsch, Louise Breski, Norm Burkeholder, Liz & Frank Files, Bonnie Gallagher, Mark Gizzi,

John & Margaritte Rowe and Fred Kerstetter.

Doug & Lisa Auclair, Craig Assimos, Rick Campbell, Victor & Alice Chiou, Alice Chen, Gang Chyi Chen, Tina Chen, Dan Detullio, Ken Gardner, Tsai-feng Hsi, Melissa Jad, Debbie Justice, Dolly Kuo, Phil & Renee Laporte, Vikki lee, Amy Liu, Chi-heng & Shu Ma Yang, Ray Mathis, Nova Montgomery & John Josetti, Donna Moran, John & Susan Parnell, Bob Pepe, Janiell Reynolds, Nancy Spadafora, Nancy Stasiak and Doris Yang.

Pete Cantone, Joan Chenworth, Andy Docus, Meredith & David Earl, Christina Sue, Ginny & Ron Hillendahl-Bueneman, Mike Hodges, Mimi & Jim Litterelle, Dan & Laura Mahoney, Patty Morasco and Susan Thomas.

Ken & Madra Christian, Fred Dowdy, Dick Cuthrell, Bonnie Forcier, Kathleen Frame, Richard Gorbety, Mark Januszewski, Pat & Penny Lafferty, Joyce May, Susan Ngo, Gary Rogers, Terry & Bob Russell, Ricky & Jackie Tysinger, Kelly & Vicki Whited, Peggy Wooten, Anthony Nguyen and John Burns.

For their unselfish support of a united industry: Eddie Lowy, Bob & Rose Rauhauser, Michael & Joan Smith, Bill Allison, Tim & Stacey Balderston, Carole Derenne, Joseph & Shane Engel, Gloria & Howard Henne, Ed & Vonna Magness, Bob Mangels, Richard Stelfox, Jackie Blasko, Sandi Kops, Russel Malehorn and Marie Ohlsson.

Also John Milton Fogg, John David Mann, Duncan Maxwell Anderson, Uma Outka, Pres Nowlin, Becki Thacker, Richard Brooke, Tom "Big Al" Schreiter, Jan Ruhe, Peggy Long, Sandy Elsberg, Glen Davidson, Kathleen Deoul, Chris and Dr. Josephine Gross, Robert Lovell, Paul Michaels, Phil Tannenholz, Elsa & George Boynton,

Vernon Brokke, David & Collie Butler, John Dealey, Thomas & Maureen Horan Entwhistle, George Fuller, Debbie Gayetty, Cherl & Victor Gonzalez, Laura Kall, Craig Keeland, Taylor Hegan, Jeannie Hopkins, Robert Larson, Ted & Ruby Lyman, Merle Miller, Keith McEachern, Warren & Mary Nelson, Shirley Pontious, Cindy Samuelson, Bob Schmidt, Eileen Silva, Collette Van Reusen, Bob Wampler, Ruth & Dennis Williams, Louise Bowman, Chuck & Claudia Branham, Cindy Burgess, James Darechuck, Steve & Lori Esrig, Ray Gebauer, Priest & Patricia Kemper, Chip Lazauskas, Edna Lawrence, Howard Schreiber, Chris Thomas, Paula Wallis, Gerald Van Yerxa, Brett Dabe, Chris & Lorraine Galloway, Roland Fox, Ed Johnson, Joe Rubino, George & Dee Dee Shaw and Ted Silverberg.

To my good friends Tim Kraft, who embodies the spirit of *Der Tuefelhunde*; Dennis O'Block, a true patriot and a Great American; and to Paul Vasold, who opened the door for me to a whole new set of adventures.

To Jim Porterfield, M.D., Julie Simon, R.N. and the thousands who sent me cards and prayers during my health challenges. Without you, I wouldn't be here.

Last, but certainly not least, are the many friends and authors of the support materials listed in Chapter 25.

There is always a danger of missing someone. I apologize for any oversight.

Finally, to my friends, family and all of the folks whose tales grace the pages of this book. Thank you for touching my life.

# Forward

Frank sent me *Reflections of a Master* as a manuscript to read. In the accompanying letter, he asked me if I'd write the Forward. "Yeah..., yeah...," I thought. I didn't want to read anybody's *Reflections...* of anything! (Arrogant and over-committed snot that I am). I just didn't want to *have to* make the time.

But it *was* Frank asking: The "Captain" (My Captain).

Funny how even from the first meeting you're always naturally inclined to say, "Yes, Sir," to Frank. (Anyone who doesn't is a damn fool!) He never Demands that kind of respect. Frank Commands it simply by being who he is: Frank Keefer— an honest-to-goodness, card carrying, been-there done-that, walking, talking Hero. And yes, he IS a Master. In my opinion, one of The Greatest Networkers in the World!

My friend, Richard Brooke (author of *Mach II With Your Hair On Fire!* And a big fan of Frank's), was staying with us for a couple of days. Richard was waiting impatiently for me to get my stuff together, so we could leave to do some recording work and had started leafing through Frank's manuscript.

"You read this?" He asked.

"Not yet," I replied

"Do it. It's a *Great* book!" Richard said.

Coming from Brooke, that's very high praise. Richard doesn't like to read books. I doubt if he's ever read his own! So, I committed to read *Reflections*. I started reading—and finished reading—the next morning. Brooke was right....

So, who is this Frank Keefer (and why should you pay any attention to his *Reflections*)…?

Frank is the most dynamic person that I've ever met. He is a living antonym.

Frank is *soft-spoken*, yet nearly everything he says is *loud*….

He is *extremely intelligent*, yet speaks *simply* and *plainly*.

He is *honest* and *direct* to a fault, and always *sensitive* and *kind*.

He has seen and done things you and I have only read about in books, or seen on TV or in a movie theatre, yet he never boasts about any of it. (though he has a right to!) Frank has long ago lost count of the number of times he's faced death, literally; the hand-to-hand, winner-takes-it-all combat kind. Yet he speaks about it all so matter-of-factly: moved to tears when he's touched by a memory, angered by injustice and waste, admiring of Duty, Sacrifice and Character.

*Character*…. Remember when we used to value *Character*…? Frank still does. In fact, *Character* is who Frank Keefer *IS*. Courage, Integrity, Wisdom, Commitment, Intelligence, Persistence, Honor, Student/Teacher, Caring, Pride…. all Frank. Sure, Go ahead and add Thrifty, Brave, Clean and Reverent. God and Country, too. Frank is a Big, Old Boy Scout—and rightfully proud of it.

Frank Keefer is the *Real Deal*—and in a world of pretenders and imposters, he's a *Rare Deal*, as well.

So enough Rah Rah about Frank—what about the book…?

*Reflections of a Master* is just what the title says it is.

I suspect you will read it as I did, cover-to-cover in one sitting. It's too compelling not to! And I also imagine you'll do the other thing that I do with this book, once you've completed the first read: You'll pull it out, fan through the pages and pick one chapter—as if by accident. And you'll read and you'll marvel at how that piece—chosen at random, just by "luck"—was exactly what you needed to "hear" at that moment.... Just the thing to move you off your butt; over, under, around or through whatever was stopping you.

*Reflections of a Master* isn't mind-chocolate. It's a manual for taking Action, and I promise, it will *Move You* to it!

Can I sum up Frank's book in a word or maybe two (after all, I'm a writer ☺...?

Yeah, I can.

*Reflections of a Master* is a book about LEADERSHIP and Frank Keefer is an INSPIRATION.

That's two. Now, It's Your Turn.

—John Milton Fogg

Author, *The Greatest Networker in the World*
www.greatestnetworker.com

# Preface

During my decades long quest for Mr. Miyagi *, I consciously paid attention to the experiences of others. I drew conclusions from their successes and failures. I benchmarked their results against my own experiences. I developed a ravenous appetite to test my hypotheses. To appease that insatiable craving, I voraciously gorged myself with life. I left few stones unturned to satisfy my hunger.

From my journey, I've drawn two conclusions:
> Life is the Study of Cause and Effect, more science
> > than art; and
> The Master is within each of us.

The conclusions in this book on values such as Courage, Honor, Integrity, Tenacity, Posture, Pride, Commitment and Service are axiomatic. They are not drawn only from the one or two anecdotes around which they are wrapped. They are validated by dozens of similar experiences that support them.

My fondest wish would be for you to go beyond what this book may offer for your network marketing business. Pick one chapter, discover the message within in that chapter, and let it change your life.

"Wax on, wax off!"*

* from the movie, *The Karate Kid*

# Introduction

# A Journey to Success

*Reflect on the message of each chapter and draw your own conclusions.*

**A dozen years ago, generic information on network marketing was scant**. To get my sales organization on the road to success, I wrote *Let's Get Down to Business*. The book was based on principles that I'd learned during fifteen years in corporate America. Since then, volumes of material have become available. Much of it centers on those approaches that I initiated over a decade ago.

I've been with four network marketing organizations. Using the principles from my original book, presented here in anecdotal form, starting from scratch each time, I have successfully hit the top pin level in the last three companies.

I don't command an annual seven-figure income, but I am in the upper 1/10 of 1% of earners. More importantly, I satisfied my goal of creating more million-dollar earners in a shorter period of time than anyone in the history of the industry. I developed my organization to be symmetrically balanced with high earners in each leg and, when I was active, my attrition was almost non-existent. My organizations have moved hundreds of millions of dollars in product. While the power of the plan is certainly significant to my success, my approach has undoubtedly played a major role.

Over the years I have been bombarded with requests to write a second book. I took a rain check until now. I was too busy having fun building my business. My intent was to be a successful network marketer, not a retailer of training aids.

Generally, I'm suspect of folks who attain a modicum of success and start pumping out "How-to" books and tapes. I have found that in many cases, there is either a need for ego gratification or a need to supplement income. I've always believed that the job of a network marketer is network marketing, not writing books.

Unfortunately, my declining health has prevented me from continuing my career with my former zealousness. I needed to do something. This book was written as a way to give back to an industry that has given so generously to me and as a way to maintain a sense of dignity through continued productivity. I have no need for ego gratification. My accomplishments speak for themselves. Nor am I looking for a supplemental source of income. Profits from this book will go to **St. Jude's Children's' Fund** and **To Blind and Paralyzed Veterans of America.**

This is not a book on techniques. "How to's" are a dime a dozen. Furthermore, this book is not intended to convince you of anything, only to get your intellectual juices flowing. Technique will carry you only so far. Without a fundamental understanding of cause and effect, you will never fully maximize your potential.

*Reflections*, therefore is a study of cause and effect. It is a presentation of information. Interpret that information anyway you wish. Whether you agree with my conclusions or not, is irrelevant. The intent is to recognize that every action produces a predictable result.

The stories are true. Exaggeration would undermine their validity. Those who know me can attest I have no need to embellish. In some anecdotes, the names may have been changed. A few of these anecdotes have appeared in edited form in other publications but their message is worth repeating.

Lest anyone reading this book misinterpret my purpose or who I am, I can assure you that I'm no superman. I'm just a regular guy who suffers from the same fears, anxieties and insecurities as everyone else. Perhaps the secret that I've learned in life is that you are only playing against yourself. Your mind can be your greatest ally or your worst enemy. You need to work, as I do on a daily basis, to cultivate that alliance.

*Reflections* is a quick read, but it is intended to be digested one chapter at a time. The chapters may be randomly selected. The content of each episode serves only as a catalyst to stimulate your thought processes on the questions and conclusions posed by that anecdote.

I suggest that you read and re-read each chapter several times before moving on to the next chapter. After each reading, pause to reflect on the intent of that chapter. Analyze and interpret the presentation. Overlay your own experiences. Draw your own conclusions. Reinforce existing beliefs or establish a new perspective. When you conclude that the topic is important enough to present a 30-60 minute presentation to your group on the message offered by that chapter, and you can outline that presentation, then you are ready to move on to another chapter.

I fear most readers will blow through the entire book in one or two sittings. That's OK, as long as you go back, re-read and devote the time necessary for in-depth analysis of each message. Otherwise, you've missed the point of the book and I've wasted my time sharing my experiences with you.

*Reflections* is a travelogue of experiences that I have enjoyed as a single man, a family man and single parent. The original manuscript contained nearly sixty chapters. My editors have advised me that any more than twenty chapters would be information overload and undermine the intent of the book. The chapters contained herein, have therefore been randomly selected although, as a result of numerous requests, several articles and editorials that I have previously written are included. The balance will be available in a second volume of a two-volume anthology.

You are about to embark on a lifetime of adventures that have revealed to me many of the secrets to success and happiness.

Our journey will be an emotional roller coaster. Together, we will experience exhilarating joy and devastating heartache. We will discover the magnificent human spirit and optimism for the future as we travel from the asphalt jungle to the blackboard jungle; from the jungles of Southeast Asia, to the jungles of Central America and South Africa; from the frozen tundra of the Arctic North to the deep blue oceans of the South Pacific; from the Tiananmen Square to the war ravaged lands of Vietnam, El Salvador, Yugoslavia (Bosnia) and Zimbabwe; from the classroom to the emergency room, from the operating room to the boardroom; from skydiving to scuba diving; from start-up businesses to Fortune Fifty companies; from entry-level sales to Corporate C.E.O; from marriage to divorce to marriage again, from being a kid to raising kids, from the first opportunity meeting to speaking before tens of thousands. It's a journey of growth. If you will open your mind, you will be changed forever.

Fasten your seatbelt. We're about to take off!

# It's Later Than You Think!

*At Some Point You Will be the Other Guy!*

**News of John Kalench's death hit me like a bullet between the eyes!** No, more like a lance through the heart. He was not only a good friend, but also an industry giant.

I have no doubt that in the short time that he was with us he accomplished his life's goal of creating a million friends. At a minimum, he changed the lives of tens of thousands through his seminars and books. I know. I was one of them. I celebrated his knowledge and experience by giving away his books by the case to both distributors and prospects as well.

Although we talked occasionally on the phone, the last time that I saw John was at a *Master's Seminar* we did in the Northwest a while back. John and I shared a common bond. The medical community had written us both off.

At the time, I was barely holding my own but miraculously John was in remission from a cancer that is fatal in nearly 100% of the cases. I was ecstatic for him.

John's passing, along with the deaths of two other friends in the same week, all three younger than me, brings to the fore front my own mortality and an adage that my uncle has drilled into my head for decades: *"It's later than you think!"*

I don't know how much time I have left. Neither do you. The difference may be that as a result of my experiences as a combat marine and later as a U.S. Army Special Forces operative coupled with seven years spent working in emergency rooms and operating rooms; I may understand it better than you do. Early on I developed a sense of urgency that I brought into my network marketing business.

If you don't have a sense of urgency, you need to develop one and you need to do it quickly! *It's later than you think!*

If you are complacent, you're defenseless. You are positioning yourself to be controlled by unforeseen circumstances in the future. Why not become proactive now and prepared for eventualities outside of your control later.

Several years back I had three folks in my organization, two personally sponsored, who were battling catastrophic illnesses. The cases were heartbreaking. None of these folks developed a sense of urgency about their business when they had the opportunity. When they became terminally ill, they were panic stricken over the financial future of their family.

Early on, before they were consumed by disease, I had encouraged them to get serious about their business. Their responses were universal. "I don't have the time." All I could do was shake my head sadly. I knew what they didn't know and didn't want to hear. *"It's later than you think!"*

Within weeks of each other they awoke one day to find that they had terminal cancer. Suddenly, faced with their own mortality, their family's financial future took on a whole new meaning. But, it was too late. They had never treated the opportunity seriously. With tears in their eyes, each came to me begging for an answer as to how they could build the business overnight.

Nothing is built overnight. This business is built showing the plan one presentation at a time, one distributor at a time. There was nothing that I could tell them.

Sacrificing a little time and money now for higher quality time and a more solid financial picture in the future was a concept that they never understood. I'd tell them that *"It's later than you think,"* but they wouldn't believe me.

Three years ago, without warning, I nearly expired due to congestive heart failure and surrounding complications. I was admitted to the hospital in critical condition with a Blood Pressure of 45/20. I was minutes from death. It took several days to get me stabilized but the damage was done. My heart muscle was irreparably trashed. I was told that it would never again operate at greater than 15%. My life expectancy was measured in weeks, a few months at best. I was told I'd never work again. My activity for evermore was not to exceed 10 minutes every other hour. I was finished!

The greatest solace to me during those dark days was that I was debt-free and had built a solid network marketing business that would not only pay me residually while I was alive, but would take care of my family after my death. Where would I have been if a few years earlier I hadn't exercised the sense of urgency necessary to build my business? Most likely, I would have been relegated to a few bucks a month of social security disability, probably would have had to sell my home and move into a low rent apartment in some seedy neighborhood and wait around to die.

You know how stuff happens to the other guy? Guess what? It happened to me! And, at some point in your life, it will happen to you. You will be the other guy. You just don't know when. In my case it was heart trouble. In John's, it was cancer. It shouldn't have happened. Both of us were physically fit and

3

nutritionally conscious. Oh well! It could just as easily have been an auto wreck, a fatal fire, random street violence or some other equally devastating situation. You're not immune. Wake up to the fact that *it's later than you think.*

You have no time to waste. Get your butt in gear! Make it happen! A successful network-marketing career is the cheapest insurance policy that you'll ever get. The premium is a little effort put forth to help others. The effort that you put forth today is your down payment for your family's security tomorrow.

*It's later than you think!*

# Basics

*Simplicity is the Key to Success.*

**I'd had a love affair with martial arts for three decades when I received an excited phone call from a friend of mine.** He was elated. I thought he'd explode!

"I just learned how to throw the reverse punch!"

The reverse punch is the most basic movement in the striking arts: karate or tae kwon do. In its most elementary form, the practitioner stands facing a mirror slightly more than arms' distance away. The feet are shoulder width apart. The arms are cocked, elbows to the rear with the fists resting on the hips, palms up. The arms are alternately shot forward at an imaginary target or reflection shoulder height and center mass. The fists are rotated during the punch, palms facing down at the symbolic moment of impact. As the striking arm is withdrawn, the resting arm shoots forward. This process of alternate striking continues ad infinitum. It's so monotonous and boring, that after a few weeks most students, failing to understand the importance of fundamentals, lose interest and discontinue training.

My friend, to the contrary, was not a student. I've trained with some of the top fighters in the world and he's among the finest I've ever known. Twenty years earlier he fought in Asia to become the full contact champion of the world. He dedicated his life to martial arts and has operated his own school for years, yet he's never lost sight of the importance of basics. Decades after being internationally recognized, he finally became expert at the most fundamental principle.

For several years I was a professional sport parachuting instructor. I started my career in teaching as a means to subsidize my own jumping. I climbed the instructional ranks: expert license, jumpmasters license, instructor rating and finally, Instructor/Examiner. By the time I became an instructor I had years of experience. Because I test jumped a number of experimental chutes, I had more parachute malfunctions and had performed more emergency procedures than anyone in the world. Most experienced jumpers had 1 or 2 malfunctions during the course of their careers. I had 18.

By studying the experiences of others, related to my own experiences, I learned firsthand to handle just about every conceivable situation. Different situations called for different responses. To give my students the best instruction possible I covered all possible malfunctions and their respective remedies.

One day I put a student with a dozen jumps out of the plane at 4500 feet. She had time for a ten second delay before opening. I watched as she plummeted to earth, passing ten, then fifteen seconds, getting smaller and smaller. I became panicky. Although she couldn't hear me, I reflexively yelled, "Pull, Pull (the ripcord)!" I was terrified she was "going in." Finally a tiny chute billowed open over a half mile below me.

After I landed, I blistered her, "Once you pass the designated freefall time (ten seconds in this case) it's no longer a sport. It's about saving your life!" She was self confident but naïve. She said, "I had a problem and I was reviewing the emergency procedures in my mind to make sure that I didn't embarrass myself by doing the wrong one."

"Whoa!" Her response hit me like an axe handle right between the eyes. I thought my classes on emergency procedures were simple but now I realized students didn't have the experience to identify situations as easily I could. I revised my class to teach only one simple, basic technique.

Network marketers too, like my martial artist friend or my skydiving student, only need one basic technique to be successful. By practicing that technique over and over again until they do it reflexively, they will develop confidence that the technique will work every time.

I have found, without question, the single most effective approach for retailing or recruiting is, "Do you know anyone who wants to lose weight (or save cash on their long distance bill, etc) or make money?"

The prospect then invariably asks, "What is it?" At that point I schedule an appointment. I don't tell them anything unless I can tell them everything. Otherwise, in their mind, they'll disqualify the opportunity or product.

That's it! Simple. It works 100% of the time.

When attending conventions, be aware of information overload. Take all of the notes you want, but pick one key point, only one, and focus on it. Drill yourself on that point until you can do it in your sleep.

Vince Lombardi took a mediocre team to the top by practicing the basics over and over again until his team was unbeatable.

You can take your business to the top by practicing basics over and over again. When you can do them reflexively and confidently, you too will be unbeatable.

7

# Becoming a Bum

*It's better than having a job!*

**Like me, Rob was a very successful corporate executive.** He was earning a healthy six-figure income, well in excess of a quarter million dollars a year. He lived in a gorgeous home that he had built on several wooded acres in an exclusive waterfront community. Both he and his wife drove luxury automobiles. And, like me, he paid the price for his success with long, hard hours. Much of it spent in airports and on the road. The cost for his financial success was higher than he realized.

Unlike me, his marriage was on the rocks. His kids were in trouble with drugs and he was working on becoming an alcoholic. Also, unlike me, he was still locked into the corporate world. I had made the transition to network marketing.

I knew that more than anything, Rob longed for a fairy tale life with his wife and kids. Because he came from a modest background, he wanted his family to enjoy the things that he had missed growing up.

In his mind, it was cast in concrete that the only way to achieve his dream was hard work in a traditional business. He had been generationally indoctrinated into believing the answer to everything was hard work in traditional business. He had focused on success like a laser beam and had successfully cut the chains of mediocrity. He hadn't realized that the price he paid was insidious. His life!

I had a moral obligation to let him know that I had found a way out.

In his back yard one Sunday afternoon, shortly before he headed out to fly cross-country, I approached him with the opportunity that had given me my life back. He immediately threw his hands in the air and with a genuinely pained expression on his face said, "Frank, Frank, Frank, I can't believe that you've allowed yourself to get sucked into one of those pyramid schemes!"

He bowed his head for a moment and shook it sadly. Then, he looked me straight in the eye, still shaking his head from side to side. "You're too smart for that. What happened to your mind? You're a well-respected corporate executive. You have everything! What about your lifestyle? I can't believe that you would give that up? Maybe you're just burned out and need a rest?"

His monologue continued with heartfelt concern.

"I had a neighbor that was just like you. He was a corporate executive doing well. Last year he made the same mistake that you're making now. He chucked a dream career to get hooked up into one of those pyramid things. He ended up turning into a bum. He grew a beard and everything. He lost his mind!"

By now Rob's intensity and conviction had me more than a little unnerved. Probably more sheepishly than I care to remember, I asked him "Did he make any money?"

"I guess so. He's still living in this neighborhood. But, all he does is hang around his house puttering in his garden and waxing his cars and stuff. He used to pay people to do those things. Now he does them himself and he doesn't appear the least bit humiliated.

And his new friends…what a collection! They all drive nice cars, but they look like bums half the time. They walk around like they haven't got a care in the world!

We never see him at the club anymore. I guess he's too embarrassed to show his face. Frank, if you don't get out fast you'll probably become a bum too!"

Rob then took his Mont Blanc pen out of his shirt pocket and on the back of one of his business cards scribbled something. "Here," he said, handing it to me. This is the name and number of the "shrink" that I'm seeing. He should be able to help you get back on the right track."

Inperceptively, I tuned Rob out. My mind started to flashback on what had happened to me since I had left corporate America and committed to network marketing:

I had no bosses. I had no employees. I had no quotas. I had no schedules. I had no office to report to. I had no stress.

I could go to bed when I wanted. I could get up when I wanted. I could spend all my time with my family. I could "putter in the garden" if I wanted. I could wax my cars if I wanted. I could go where I wanted and do what I wanted, when I wanted. Nobody owned me.

I was earning an income that exceeded my corporate income. I had become totally debt-free. I could walk into any store that I wanted and buy anything that I wanted without looking at a price tag. The checks came in every week whether I worked or not. If I felt like working, I could work at home in my underwear.

I had helped dozens of people cut the chains of economic bondage by becoming debt-free. From the company that I represented, I had the opportunity to purchase a multitude of first class products wholesale. The cost of all my travel and entertainment was cut in half as a result of legitimate tax deductions.

I had a new circle of friends too. They, like me, could come and go as they pleased. Lifestyle? It was never better. I experienced not only material fulfillment, but also emotional satisfaction and freedom from worry.

Then it dawned on me, Rob was right. I hadn't gotten out fast enough. I'd become a bum!

# 4

# Irritating the Neighbors

*You don't have to be a Drug Dealer!*

**One morning a few years ago, I received an urgent call from Pete.** His voice radiated a sense of concern. He was insistent that I meet with him immediately. We'd served together in the military. Although it wasn't true, Pete was convinced that I'd saved his life in combat. Pete was a police officer.

At the time, my wife Gingie and I lived in a rundown 200-year-old mansion. Residing on an eminence east of town, *L'Alhambra* offered a commanding and spectacular view of the Patapsco River Valley and Ellicott Mills; a quaint hamlet that resembles a Christmas garden nestled snugly in a thickly forested, granite valley. The town's rich history predated the Revolutionary War. It was the site of the first railroad terminus in the world. It had been occupied by Union troops during the War Between the States. During WWI, the town's mill had supplied the uniforms worn by the Doughboys. At one time, it was the honeymoon capital of the East Coast.

In spite of *L'Alhambra's* deplorable condition, we were captivated by visions of restoring it to its original grandeur. It would take a lot of work. At various times it had served as a brothel and a motorcycle gang hangout.

Restoration was tedious. It took three years to clean the front yard of broken beer bottles. Neighbors often stopped by. With pride they would congratulate us on our rehabilitation.

Around that time, I left corporate America and became a network marketer. Because I was home everyday, I had more time to tend to the rehab. As the facelift became more pronounced, there was a noticeable change in the attitude of my neighbors. The better our home looked, the more apparent the tension became. I was at a loss as to why. Friction turned to hostility.

Although I couldn't put my finger on it, I felt a definite sense of suspicion on the part of my neighbors. I was flabbergasted.

Then I received Pete's call. I met him for breakfast at a local diner. He sat across the table, his eyes peering intently into mine. His face was ashen. "I owe you one from Vietnam," he said. "I could lose my job over this, maybe even go to jail. If you're involved in the sale of illegal drugs, clean up your act ASAP!"

"Whoa!" My eyebrows hit the ceiling! His comments caught me completely off guard!

"Involved in the sale of illegal drugs? Are you out of your mind? That's the most ridiculous thing I've ever heard. Why are you asking me a question like that?"

Pete breathed a noticeable sigh of relief, but he blew my mind when he announced I was under investigation for the distribution of illegal substances.

"Why?" I asked.

"Your neighbors reported you."

"You've got to be kidding? On what basis?" I was totally puzzled.

"You no longer leave for work in the morning and you have no visible means of support.

14

You've been observed spending most of your time at home floating in your pool talking on the telephone.

In spite of the fact that you're no longer employed, you're obviously spending a lot of money because of the number of contractors working at your place and the extensive restoration work being done.

You have a continual stream of bizarre characters showing up at your house at all hours of the day and night. The fact that they're driving everything from Cadillacs to beat up pick up trucks is a bit strange and certainly suspect.

You own more cars than one person needs and they're all top of the line. That, plus your license plates really aroused their suspicions. You remind them of the drug dealers on *Miami Vice*. Given the other information, those plates would raise a red flag for me."

"My license plates?"

"Yeah. Drug dealers like to flaunt their status. Your tags say it all: PDCASH, NODEBT and LIFSTYL. But what's this 'McTAMER'? Nobody can figure that one out?"

'McTAMER'? Oh you mean MKTAMER (Market America). That's the company I represent as an independent distributor. It's a home-based business and perfectly legal.

"And you can make the same type of money as drug dealers? No job pays that much?"

"Oh yeah? We need to talk. Not only can you earn as much as you want, but the lifestyle that you can create through network marketing does a lot more than that. It'll give you the time freedom to do what you want, when you want and have as much

15

fun as you want."

"That lifestyle does something else, too."

"Oh yeah, what's that, Pete?"

"It irritates the neighbors!"

# 5

# Courage

*Sometimes, the Greatest Acts of Heroism unfold Only Over Time.*

**The summer night was as black as pitch.** In spite of the gently falling precipitation, there was no humidity. The air was comfortably cool. Against the lush green vegetation the rhythmic pattering of rain provided soothing, almost hypnotic, background music. In another time, in another place this would have been the ideal setting to drift off into a peaceful sleep. But, this was Vietnam, 1965.

Suddenly, without warning, blinding flashes and the concussion of incoming mortars split the tranquility like a ripe melon. White-hot shrapnel saturated the air. Incoming green tracers punctuated the darkness as a numerically superior enemy assaulted and breached friendly lines. The response was the detonation of claymore mines.

Within minutes illumination rounds burst overhead. Their parachute flares, lazily descending, bathed the ground in a macabre kaleidoscope of light while the alternating whistle of their metal canisters plummeting to earth signaled yet another obstacle to survival. Orange tracers spewed forth from returning automatic weapons fire contributing to a pyrotechnic display that would have shamed the best 4th of July celebration.

Held close to the ground by the light rain, the acrid stench of burning cordite was suffocating. Amidst the chattering of machine guns young men on both sides barked orders. Others screamed like banshees. The cacophony of sound was deafening. Cold steel met warm bodies as warriors locked in mortal combat. The terror was unimaginable. The permanence of death became instant reality.

An enemy grenade landed in the midst of a small group of defenders. Without hesitation, James Reilly dove on top of the sputtering missile absorbing the full impact of the explosion with his own body. He had saved his comrades at the cost of his own life.

I could fill volumes with first hand accounts of such heroics. But, I learned long ago that the greatest tests of courage are not limited solely to physical acts that arise from a sense of immediacy. Those whose resolve remains stalwart in the face of great personal challenges or emotional distress also exhibit incredible courage.

I felt an unbelievable sense of emptiness at the recent loss of Henry Herold; a high school chum with whom I enlisted. I filled that void with reflections of his lifetime of courage.

Henry was the first of us to be seriously wounded. After evacuation to Japan and recuperation, he voluntarily returned to action. He felt an obligation to his buddies. Within weeks, he was seriously wounded again. This time he was evacuated to the states.

After recovery, at a time when public sentiment was often "those killed in Vietnam got what they deserved", he was assigned the gut wrenching duty of escorting home the remains of those killed in action; and, as a 20 year old Marine, tasked to explain to grieving parents why their son had died. The courage necessary to face such a challenge is mind boggling and rarely appreciated. Most will never relate to the emotional toughness needed to survive such a mission.

As a Baltimore City Police Officer his courage was tested often over the next three decades; but he may have experienced his toughest challenge when he was unexpectedly widowed a few years ago. Metaphorically he threw himself on a hand grenade of despair and smothered his own grief to become an instrument of strength for his kids. Henry was a hero.

A former business associate lettered in four sports in college. At age 22 he was crushed from the pelvis down in a horrific automobile accident. Not only was he robbed of his athleticism but he was never expected to walk again. His trauma so impaired his circulation that, to the touch, his lower extremities felt like the cold marble of a museum statue. It was anticipated that his feet would eventually become necrotic and require amputation.

Now, nearly thirty years later, miraculously, he is ambulatory. His success is not just a consequence of countless operations or years of rehabilitation but a result of decades of massaging his feet for two and a half hours a day, day after day, week after week, year after year. Folks who have never experienced the need to perform such a tedious regimen can't appreciate the incredible tenacity that it takes to keep from becoming emotionally whipped and throwing in the towel. He is also a hero.

The alcoholic who dries out and stays sober, the junkie who kicks heroin and stays clean, the spouse who leaves an abusive marriage after years of suffering and the blind, the deaf and the terminally ill who spit in the eye of adversity are also heroes. They testify that the truest test of courage, the ultimate act of heroism, is the willingness to make a decision to live a purposeful life and the resolve to stick with it, regardless of obstacles.

Make no mistake; it takes courage to change your life. You displayed the seeds of courage necessary for financial freedom by starting your own home based business but do you have the guts to stay the course, or will you wimp out when the going gets tough? The choice is yours.

Perseverance, that's the real difference between a hero and a coward!

# 6

# Choice

*America's Greatest Gift.*

**I absolutely loved football!** How could I help it? I came of age in the 50's during the heyday of the Baltimore Colts. In those days professional athletes didn't command obscene salaries. Their incomes were on a par with our fathers, but only if they worked off-season, selling tires at Sears, tending bar or peddling insurance. Suburban sprawl had not yet begun its malignant growth. Cities were confined to their geographic boundaries. The players lived in our neighborhoods. On Saturdays we'd go to the barbershop to watch our heroes get their haircut. I wanted to be like them. I wanted to play football!

When I was 13, for the first time ever, a kids' football league was formed. Every kid in the neighborhood rushed to join. My parents wouldn't sign for me. I was heartbroken.

In high school I worked full time. Playing football was not an option. In a school with 4000 boys I didn't believe that I'd make the cut anyway. I didn't realize then that skill is only half of the equation. Heart makes up the rest. My heart had not matured to the point where it made any difference. It wasn't until the Marine Corps that I learned that spirit could potentiate skill.

I was stationed in California in the early 60's. One fall afternoon the Colts came to L.A. to play the Rams. I waited outside of the coliseum. When the bus arrived I went up to a 33-year-old coach named Don Schula, told him I was from Baltimore and asked if he could get me in to see the game. I

21

went in with the team through their dressing room. I sat behind the bench. Some day I would sit on that bench.

I wanted to play ball in college but my schedule and financial situation didn't allow it. During that time, I worked for a Hall of Famer. I wrangled sideline seats whenever possible. The players were tough, but no tougher than me; and, for the most part, no bigger. I was quick and could absorb a tremendous amount of punishment. There was no doubt in my mind that I could make the team as a 'walk on'.

Sometime, between graduation and my "tryout," I made my first skydive.

I had been a paratrooper but had never free fallen. Sport parachuting was in its infancy. There were no training centers. Jumping was a matter of finding someone with a plane and an obliging farmer with an open field. The rig de jour was military surplus. The sport was made for me. I hit the silk everyday. I became known as a "serious jumper."

By the time the next football season came around I was doing 60 second freefalls (that's a 2 mile freefall) at 120-200 mph. I had learned to soar a mile laterally for every 2 miles I freefell vertically. I was in the forefront of learning how to fly my body to link up with others to create aerial formations in freefall. No doubt, I would make the U.S. Team!

It was either football or skydiving. I made a choice.

It's impossible to verbalize my passion for jumping. It became part of my livelihood. I was one of the top rated jumpers in the world. Hollywood offered me a job as stunt double for one of the leading stars of the time. Suddenly, I was blindsided by divorce.

I believed I had the perfect marriage when my wife announced she was moving 1000 miles away. I would be excommunicated from my kids. I was devastated. I was a war orphan and had never known my Dad. Being a father was the most important thing in the world to me. Custody for men in those days was unheard of. I had absolutely no chance at all if I continued skydiving.

It was either a shot at the U.S. Parachute Team or my kids? I made a choice.

Fast-forward 20 years. I had climbed the corporate ladder. By all accounts I was successful. I was earning over a quarter of a million dollars annually. I had my own secretary. I was autonomous. I could afford to take my family around the world and go skiing several times a year. I didn't think that life couldn't get any better.

One day, shortly after a family ski trip, my bride presented me with a photo album of our vacation. It consisted of forty pictures of me on the telephone with clients. I was missing the boat and hadn't realized it.

In Jamaica, at a President's Club Convention for top executives, a colleague told me about network marketing. I saw the leverage immediately but it was the chance for commensurate income with unencumbered family time that attracted me.

It was either a prestigious corporate career or some crazy "pyramid scheme" that offered freedom. I made a choice.

What about you? Whether you are in a traditional career or network marketing, you're either getting what you want out of life or you're not.

Make a choice!

# 7

# Turning Green

*On Sea, In the Air or in your Mind!*

**Life aboard a troopship at sea during the mid 60's was reminiscent of a WWII documentary.** Twelve hundred combat marines and two hundred sailors were crammed aboard the vessel like sardines. The deck was covered by the same landing craft that had stormed the beaches at Tarawa and Iwo Jimo. Attached to the gunwales were massive cargo nets ready to unroll over the side for troops to climb down and disembark into landing barges.

Ship life was austere at best. But, if it was good enough for our fathers, it was good enough for us. We felt like we were part of history. Every ship I sailed had been commissioned prior to 1940. Sleeping compartments were about the size of a townhouse living room. These compartments held about 45 marines. Each slept on a 2'X6'piece of canvas lashed to a slightly larger rectangular pipe known as a "rack." Racks were stacked six high, two rows deep and eight across. There was 2 ½ feet separating them vertically and horizontally. Each troop with all his gear was confined to one tiny berth. There was no wasted space.

Usually there was only one entrance, a hatch in the overhead (ceiling) the size of a manhole cover. Ventilation was non-existent. If one guy puked, everybody got sick. The saltwater showers were terrible. You always felt stickier afterwards. There were no toilets, only a trough of running seawater and a nearby box of wooden slats. You'd grab two for a makeshift seat and lay them across the trough hoping the ship didn't hit any swells.

The mess hall only held about forty troops at one time. Life was a continuous chow line. Eat and get back in line for the next meal.

In August 1965, we hit a ten-day typhoon in the South Pacific. The magnificence of this seaborne hurricane was incomprehensible. The movie *Perfect Storm* doesn't come close to conveying the omnipotence Mother Nature displayed that week. The unsophisticated, phony-looking special effects of 1940's movies using a toy boat in a bathtub were a more accurate depiction. Mountainous waves could have swallowed the ship in one gulp. The saltiest veterans were sick. It was the first time I'd ever seen everybody around me actually turn green.

The second time was aboard a C130 air transport. Over a hundred paratroops, each encumbered with chutes, rifles and 75 pounds of gear were jammed in the hull of the aircraft for a tactical training exercise. We flew for over 24 turbulent hours, refueling in flight.

There were four rows of nylon mesh benches attached to metal frames running the entire length of the aircraft: two in the center each facing outboard and one each on either side of the aircraft facing inboard. Troops sat facing each other. Once seated and belted in, it was impossible to move. There were no bathroom facilities. There was no interior insulation. Condensation would alternately freeze on the inside skin of the aircraft or melt, dripping either rain or sleet on the troops depending on the temperature which could vary 40°F or 50°F. It was like being in a combination steam bath/igloo. The air was stagnant. Everyone was sick from fatigue and lack of food.

Some idiot lit up a cigar. One of the troopers puked. The effect was cataclysmic. Motion sickness bags and berets were

26

immediately filled with stomach contents. The stench was unbearable. As though a switch was flipped, simultaneously everyone took on a greenish hue, which radiated throughout the aircraft.

The third time I saw an entire group turn green was several years ago while doing a seminar on goal setting. Things went along well until I made no bones about the fact that the attendees would be required to design a detailed plan for their future before they left the room. No exceptions! They were terrorized. I could visibly see their color change, first to ashen and then green. I couldn't believe that some of them were actually getting sick.

The thought that I would hold them accountable for planning their own future was too much. Success just offered too many options for them to deal with. They were so used to being told what to do that, left to their own thought processes, they became dysfunctional. They reminded me of the school kid told to write a composition for homework. He forgets about it until right before class the next day. Suddenly, he remembers! He panics for a minute but if he's been given a topic, e.g. what he did during the summer or his father's occupation, he can B.S. his way through it. If he hasn't been given a specific topic, he becomes paralyzed, unable to think on his own. He ends up with a zero.

The same thing is true with people's futures. You're told to work until 65, retire and die. The thought that you can be or do something on your own is too incomprehensible for most people to even think about It's easier to be a rudderless ship.

Do yourself a favor. Take a Dramamine. Plan your future. You'll end up with rosy cheeks!

# 8

# Perception is Reality

*In the Mind of the Beholder.*

**While I certainly had the credentials**, I had been unable to gain admission to medical school. Grasping at straws, I enrolled in Nursing School. I naively believed that somehow I could leverage that degree into boosting my chances for admittance. It wasn't long before I found that my experience as medic and pharmacologist far exceeded the nursing curriculum.

I was thirty years old, as were most of the other students. About 98% were women. Because the perception at that time called into question the gender preference of any male who entered the nursing profession, few men attended. This created a problem, particularly in the hospitals. Student nurses were required to wear hideous looking uniforms to prevent them from being misidentified as "real Nurses". There was no such costume for men. Instead, we wore lab coats, but with a nametag that identified us as a student nurses.

In spite of my persistence to establish my true status, patients constantly referred to me as "Doctor." It wasn't just the coat; it was my self-confidence as a result of my previous medical experience. One day, immediately after I had explained to an elderly lady that I was a student, a nursing instructor came in and heard the patient refer to me as Doctor. The instructor went ballistic. The elderly patient looked at me and said, "Don't pay any attention to her, Doctor. It's probably her time of the month."

Because of my broad medical background, students often came

up to me with medical questions rather than go to the instructors who often had little practical experience or who would belittle them. This created a perception among the staff that I was trying to usurp their authority. Nothing could have been farther from the truth. It was the farthest thing from my mind.

A few years before nursing school, I was in scrub clothes at City Hospital. I was introducing a new and very powerful intravenous muscle relaxant. My job was to assist anesthesiologists in the operating room by monitoring dosage schedules. Gurneys jammed the hallways with pre-op patients, mostly emergency cases. One young man beckoned me over. He was terrified. He was the victim of an abdominal gunshot wound. His intestines were protruding from his abdominal wall. "Am I going to die, Doc?" he said. "I'm not a physician," I responded. "Sure you are," he answered hesitantly. Then he pleaded, "Please don't let me die alone, Doc." I held his hand for an hour until the staff could get to him.

These stories illustrate that whether it's being gay, being a physician or having some hidden agenda to gain control over others, whether it's true or not, perception is reality in the eyes of the beholder.

The saddest example of perception being reality may be race relations. If you believe the media, most blacks perceive that the majority of whites to be racists. If that were true why did polls show that Colin Powell would have garnered 80% of the white vote in the recent presidential election, a higher percentage than for either white candidate? Why is Oprah Winfrey, TV's highest paid star, so beloved in the white community? What adult doesn't envy the parents of Tiger Woods? But, if racism's the perception, it's the reality in the mind of the believer.

Stereotypes, whether positive or negative, blend perception into reality. There is a stereotypical belief about network marketing. The Direct Selling Association found most folks have a negative opinion about network marketing even though they admit they don't know anyone who is a network marketer. From fifth hand sources they've heard terms like "pyramid scheme." They perceive scam and that perception becomes reality.

How do we change perception? It starts within us. What are our perceptions? Do we believe, I mean really believe, way down deep inside, that network marketing is a solid and legitimate business, one that we are proud to be part of. Do we really believe that everyone we bring in can succeed? Do we believe that we will succeed? Whether we do or we don't, that perception becomes our reality. That reality is then passed along as a perception to others, prospects and distributors, and it becomes reality in their eyes.

I have a very close friend in the business who's made millions. She's sharp as a tack now, but very early on, she didn't have a clue what she was doing. But, because she believed that she would succeed, her perception became her reality. That reality was contagious to all who came in contact with her and she built a huge, highly successful organization.

In my organization, I flat out told people that they would succeed if they followed the blueprint for success. They believed me. I created the perception and it became their reality.

You are where you are in your business because of what you believe. Nurture a positive belief by attending seminars, listening to tapes, using the products that give you the best results and, most importantly, by associating with positive

# Driving a Cab

# 9

*Follow your Plan with Conviction!*

**In 1967 life on campus was brutal for returning veterans.** I made a decision to blow through college in two years instead of four. I was paying my own way. Doubling my class load dramatically increased my already overwhelming financial burden. My schedule revolved around both day and evening classes. It was tough to find accommodating employment. A fellow student suggested driving a cab. It made sense.

The university was located in the city. I reasoned that I could log a few hours between classes during the day, park my cab in the evening, pop in for a night class or two, then go back to work.

Even then, driving a cab in Baltimore City, particularly at night, was risky business. My friends were concerned about my safety.

One of my more significant experiences occurred one night as I drove by the Greyhound Bus Station. Two elderly ladies of color hailed me. As I pulled over, three young thugs, also of color, shoved one old lady aside, and in their haste to board my cab, knocked the other one down. Outwardly I maintained my composure. Inwardly, I went ballistic.

I am a War Orphan from WWII. My grandmothers had a significant role in my formative years. I dearly loved them. As I looked out of the window of my cab, I saw my grandmothers being abused and disrespected. I wanted to teach these punks a lesson.

One hopped in the front seat, the other two in the back. As I drove away, their actions confirmed they were up to no good. In the rear view mirror I could catch their eyes nervously darting back and forth. I could hear the slightest tinge of apprehension in their voices. They directed me out of the city to a secluded spot. Because we were leaving the city far behind, there was no doubt that they were going to steal my cab after they robbed me. Otherwise, they'd be stranded. I had them right where I wanted them.

Although I was certainly apprehensive, the farther out of town we drove, the harder it was for me to keep from smiling. I knew what was on their minds. They didn't have a clue what was on mine.

They had given me the name of a fictitious destination with directions that had taken us about ten miles from the city. We were on a desolate road when they told me to pull over. Although I acted naively about the events that I suspected were about to unfold, I confidently told them that the place that we were looking for was a little farther down the road. Incredibly, they didn't challenge me. I went another five miles. We were so far outside of town now that you couldn't even see the glow of city lights in the night sky.

They anxiously told me to pull over to the side of the road and stop. I did. No doubt they were armed but I acted first. In a split second I reached under my lap and withdrew a .25 Caliber Beretta, a handgun small enough to fit in my palm. I shoved it in the face of the thug in the passenger seat while I focused on the far passenger on the right in the back. I could see all three peripherally. The last thing that I wanted to do was hurt anyone, but I positioned myself to shoot from left to right if necessary.

I had caught them totally off guard. I ordered them out of the cab and face down on the ground. I had to bite my lip to keep from laughing as I announced with great bravado, "I'm just back from Vietnam and I'll shoot all three of you between the eyes in less than two seconds if any of you move before I'm out of sight." It sounded like a script from some ridiculous "B" Movie.

Before I pulled away, I gave them their final marching orders! "If I ever see or hear of you knocking any old ladies down again, I'm going to come looking for you. The next time you won't be so lucky!" One hundred percent fabrication, but what a lesson!

As I drove the 15 miles back to town, I chuckled at the thought of the blisters they would grow during their long walk back. I hoped they'd learned something.

Little did I realize that the lessons I learned that night would save me from an assassination attempt two decades later. I was a civilian military advisor in Central America when a double agent caught me unarmed and put a pistol to my head. I thought about the cab incident as I was about to be executed. Those previous experiences that saved my life that night are the same ones that I would use years later to build a successful network marketing business.

What are those lessons?

Adversaries, as well as prospects, often show their hand, telegraphing what they are thinking. If you learn to listen, you'll pick this up. You'll know what's on their mind, but if you remain stoic, you won't signal your own plan of action. This will give you the decided advantage, particularly while prospecting. It offers you the opportunity to go on the offensive and take preemptive action. Does this make sense?

Relax, compose yourself, mentally map out your strategy and follow your plan with posture and conviction.

Keep in mind too, that you will maximize your success if you go the extra five miles!

# 10

# How Will You Be Remembered?

*Honor is the Foundation of Leadership.*

**Duty, Honor, Country. These words, like *integrity* and *leadership*, are bandied around so loosely today that they have lost almost all meaning.** Not to me, and I hope not to you.

While recently rummaging through some boxes I came across a program from the most prestigious of the Presidential Inaugural Balls, the *Salute to Heroes*. This Inaugural Ball is reserved exclusively for recipients of the Congressional Medal of Honor, the Nation's most distinguished award for valor. The year was 1985. The Ball was in celebration of Reagan's election to a second term and I was honored to be a guest of the Medal of Honor Society.

Most Medals of Honor are presented posthumously, and the awards are received, not won. Today there are only about 150 surviving recipients in this elite group. They represent WWI, WWII, Korea, Vietnam, Somalia and other lesser-known engagements.

Across the board, the recipients project humility. They rarely acknowledge their own deeds, passing off the recognition that they have received as being representative of the duty performed by many.

This was neither my first nor only association with these selfless individuals, several of whom are as close as family.

When we visit, we rarely discuss combat. When we talk seriously we occasionally talk about personal dedication to *duty, honor and country,* the commitment of the Founding Fathers and the dedication of our lives to a higher purpose than self-gratification. Few are better qualified to discuss such subjects than those whose actions have demonstrated their commitment to others at the risk of their own lives.

Two autographs on the front of the program catapulted me into a state of deep reflection. Both signatories, friends of mine, passed away this year: Marine Force Recon Sergeant Major Jimmie Howard and Army Special Forces Master Sergeant Roy Benavidez. Boldly emblazoned under each signature were the words *Duty, Honor and Country.*

Their citations, which can be found on the web, don't come close to telling their stories.

Marine recon Sergeant Jimmy Howard, a gentle giant, was shot and bayoneted when Chinese communists overran his unit during the Korean War. He was decorated for valor for saving his unit from decimation during that action. Fifteen years later while leading an eighteen man recon team in Vietnam, his squad was cut off and surrounded by an enemy force that numbered in the hundreds. He and his men retreated to a small hilltop where they formed a tight defensive perimeter. Fierce fighting raged as the enemy attempted to overrun his position. During the savage hand-to-hand combat that followed that night, all but one of his team were killed or wounded numerous times. Nearly out of ammo, he instructed his team to use catcalls, laughter and war whoops to psyche out his foe. Then, to make every shot count, the team, at his direction, threw rocks at the enemy. The enemy mistook the rocks for grenades and frantically sought cover exposing themselves as targets. The survivors, surrounded by scores of dead enemy soldiers, had nine rounds (bullets) left when rescued the next day.

Green Beret Sergeant Roy Benavidez volunteered for a suicide rescue mission to aid a recon team that had been overrun and nearly wiped out by a numerically superior enemy force. During insertion, his helicopter came under intense enemy fire and was shot down killing or severely wounding all of the rescuers. Although dazed as a result of the crash, he began searching the area for his comrades and dragged their unconscious bodies to a rallying point. During the action he was severely wounded numerous times by hand grenades and small arms fire. As he continued his rescue efforts, he was shot several more times. Finally, the enemy overwhelmed him. He was struck in the face with a rifle butt that broke his jaw and knocked out his teeth. He was then bayoneted. Refusing to die, he managed to dispatch his assailant with a knife before killing two more enemy soldiers and continuing the rescue. Upon evacuation, he passed out from loss of blood and was left with the dead for hours before someone noticed that he still clung to life.

What does this have to do with Network Marketing? Simply this, to enhance the professional image of our industry, we must embody the same spirit of duty as these honorable men. Our task is certainly nowhere near as daunting as what Jimmy or Roy faced.

General Norman Schwarzkopf of Gulf War fame once shared with me his secret to success, which he believes applies to all occupations. Simply put: "Do the right thing." I would add, do the right thing with graciousness and humility.

Several years ago Gingie and I spent some time in private conversation with Senator John McCain who had been brutally mistreated as a POW in North Vietnam. This was before John became a nationally prominent politician. The conversation was light but when it was time to leave, to acknowledge his past ordeal, I said simply, "John, I appreciate your service."

I caught him off guard. He was obviously surprised that I knew of his ordeal. He seemed embarrassed.

To this day I get a lump in my throat when I recall the sincerity and humility in his voice as he replied: "It was my pleasure to serve."

Honor is the foundation of leadership. Success or failure is dependent upon leadership; therefore honor, or the lack of it, is the ingredient behind the end result.

What limits success is a lack of leadership? What limits leadership is lack of character? Even the most cunning of moral eunuchs will be found out in time. Likewise, time will validate honorable intentions. People of honor accept the fact that they may suffer some bruises before honor prevails.

Leaders must have higher standards than their followers. They must set the example. They must step up to the plate and accept responsibility. They know they will never achieve their true measure of success if they remain as followers. They must learn to place the success of the mission above personal success. They must have confidence that by feeding the troops first, by taking care of their people, they will be successful.

There is reason why service academies teach that a cadet or midshipman doesn't lie, cheat or steal or tolerate those who do. The Academies recognize that without honor one will never be a true leader.

Are you a leader? Do you act in good faith towards others without reservation? Is your word your bond? Do you hold yourself and others to a moral code or do you excuse yourself or others for moral irresponsibility? Finally, are your decisions based on self-interest or do you place the interests of others first?

In business as in life, your actions, more than your words, will be remembered long after you are gone.

# 11

# Posture

*Teaching in the City.*

**It was the late 60's. The war in Southeast Asia was going full blast.** Political unrest and social turmoil were virulent. The times had given birth to the militant Weathermen and the Black Panthers. I was completing my last course before graduation: student teaching.

With heightened social conscience, my fellow classmates, most from the lily-white suburbs, requested assignments to the inner city where they could fulfill their evangelical zeal of saving society.

I'd grown up in the city. I opted for a cushy position at some county school. Based on my academic standing, I would be given preference. The assignments were dispensed. I was surprised to find that it was I who went to the city. My classmates went to the suburbs.

I dearly admired the Chairman of the Education Department, Dr. Henry, a soft-spoken mountain of a man who reminded me of a black John Wayne. He pulled me aside, "Frank, we need you in the city. These other folks wouldn't last five minutes." I saluted smartly.

Ironically, I was assigned to the same all male high school that I'd attended years earlier. The school boasted a rich tradition that dated to 1839. The facility was a huge, turn-of-the century Gothic structure reminiscent of a medieval castle. The impressive alumnae roster included nationally prominent athletes, authors, businessmen, high government officials and entertainment celebrities. The staff included attorneys, physicians, politicians and sports celebrities. Many had seen combat service in WWII or Korea, a few in WWI. They were addressed as Professor. They had one stated mission, to produce "gentlemen."

During the era that I attended, aberrant behavior was not tolerated. Infringements were often rewarded with a trip to the gym and a chance to display one's boxing skill; but freedoms matched the uncompromising discipline. Leaving the school grounds for lunch or running errands was OK, but cutting class was verboten. Smoking was allowed during fire drills and in some classes; littering the ground with butts wasn't. Alcohol was accepted at school dances. Drunkenness was not.

The student population was 4000 when I attended. The demographics had migrated from a mixed racial bag, 1/3 Gentile, 1/3 Jewish and 1/3 Black to 2000 students, 95% of whom were Black. Times had changed but the core values taught by that great institution had not. I did my best to emulate those Professors who had shaped my life.

My host teacher soon disappeared. I became a full time U.S. History teacher. I respected my students, but ran class like boot camp. I established my persona and set the standard immediately. I'd learned in the military, that command presence, once lost, is never recovered.

With the exception of one young man, discipline problems had been preemptively eliminated. He was not one of the "toughs," but one of the brighter kids out to make a name for himself.

Several times he verbally backed me into a corner. Enough was enough. I excused myself from class and invited him to accompany me next door to the book room. While entering the room his head was accidentally caught between the heavy oaken door and the jamb. He returned to class dizzy but subdued.

The next day, prior to the start of class, the biggest black man that I'd ever seen met me in the hall. There was fire in his eyes and so much anger in his voice that I couldn't understand his dialect. I finally realized he intended to sit in the back of the room and "observe class."

Class started. I immediately recognized the resemblance between Mr. Wise Guy, sitting up front grinning like a Cheshire cat, and the guest in the back, obviously his older brother. Suddenly, there was no doubt in my mind why he was really there! I was dead meat! What was I going to do?

I could run away, call for assistance or duke it out with him—a contest I wouldn't win. I understood the code of the asphalt jungle. Exercising any of those options would trumpet the end of my teaching career. On the streets or in the classroom, there was no room for cowards or losers.

I made my plan. The entrance to the room was at the rear, the exit at the front. No class was coming in next period. The back door would remain closed. As quickly as possible, I'd scoot the kids out the front door and close it behind them. As long as the students didn't see me get my butt kicked, I would still be "good to go."

My desk sat on a raised platform. After clearing the room of the students, I would pick up my heavy oak chair, swing around, and, as he charged me, smack him with it and run out the front door. The hall would be cleared by then. No one would see me bolt; therefore, I wouldn't be compromised. Discretion is always the better part of valor.

This might be my last class. I was going to make it my best. Once or twice the wise guy acted up. I shut him down immediately. I wasn't going out like a wimp.

The bell rang. I shooed the students out the front door, closed it behind them, spun around and grabbed the chair ready to blast the older brother. I didn't see him! I panicked! "Where was he hiding?" It took me a few seconds to realize he'd left by the back door while I was ushering the class out of the front door. I was puzzled as to why he left, but that bewilderment didn't stop my sigh of relief at having escaped serious bodily harm.

I didn't see Mr. Wise Guy until the following Monday. He looked like he'd fallen into a cement mixer. He was quiet as a church mouse the rest of the year.

I learned later that his older brother had determined that it was he, not I, who was the problem.

The lesson here? Even with my backside on the line, I didn't buckle in front of the class. I didn't hesitate to take the wise guy to task even in front of his brother. That doesn't mean that I'm brave. It means the alternative, humiliating myself in front of the class, was far less desirable.

As it turned out, my posture not only saved my butt, but also established me as an effective teacher with the brother and with the rest of the class. That same carriage has enabled me to become an effective network marketer.

How about you? Does your presence in front of prospective distributors project total conviction? Is your self-confidence rock-solid as you approach prospects; or, are you timid? Do you buckle when objections are raised or are you self-assured? Are you proud or embarrassed to announce that you are a network marketer?

Your success is a barometer of your posture. Work on establishing posture! It's more desirable than the humiliating alternative.

# 12

# Instilling Confidence

*Sometimes it takes a Little Push!*

**Fred Stephans was the best skydiving instructor I'd ever seen.** His self-confident and easy-going manner made him a natural. Nobody was better at relaxing students prior to their first parachute jump than Fred.

The typical aircraft was a single-engine Cessna. Except for the pilot's seat, everything was stripped from the interior. The jump door, on the right side of the plane, opened at the bottom, swung upwards and locked parallel to the wing. There was a step above the wheel, directly below the strut.

Students entered the plane in reverse order of exit. The jumpmaster entered last and sat on the floor adjacent to the pilot, facing rearward. At 1000' the jumpmaster opened the door to get his bearings as the plane spiraled upwards to 3000', jump altitude.

On jump run, the jumpmaster did a last minute inspection of the student's equipment and attached the static line, which automatically deployed the chute, to a "D" ring on the floor. On the jumpmaster's order, the pilot throttled back to reduce air speed. The student climbed out, put his feet on the step, faced the direction of flight and held onto the strut. At the precise exit spot, the jumpmaster smacked the student on the rump, pointed down and yelled, "Go!" The student would then spring rearward, arching his back going from a vertical standing position to a horizontal belly-to-earth position, head high

49

watching the plane as he fell away. The end of the static line attached to the chute was S-folded across the backpack and held in place by rubber bands. As the jumper fell, the static line, attached to the apex of the canopy would pay out until the chute was fully deployed out of the pack. At that point a 20 lb test cord attached to the canopy would break, severing the student's attachment to the plane. The chute would then fill with air and inflate allowing the jumper to float safely to earth.

Rick, a student the size of John Wayne, was an aspiring jumper in his early 30's. He was also deaf and dumb. Using pen and paper, Fred patiently conveyed the information necessary for Rick to make a safe parachute jump. Intermittently, he confirmed Rick's understanding of all procedures.

Jump day came. On the ground we heard the aircraft cut its engine back indicating a student run. Instinctively we looked up and waited for the billowing chute to open. Nothing happened. The plane continued its circular run making three more passes, each time, hanging a student in the breeze. The fifth pass was a repeat of the first. Nothing happened.

When the plane landed, Fred said Rick had climbed out twice but refused to go. As Area Safety Officer, I reminded Fred of the danger of students getting out on the strut, not jumping and then climbing back into the plane. This excessive movement could precipitate an accidental parachute deployment that could entangle in the rudder or tail wing, causing a crash and the death of everyone on board.

Rick went up again. It was a repeat performance. Fred and I had jumpmastered hundreds of students without incident. Although he didn't show it, I'm sure Fred was professionally embarrassed.

Rick showed up again the following week. The plane flew over several times. Nothing happened. Rick again! Angry jumpers on the ground waiting their turn to jump gave me the evil eye. I was not happy.

I blurted out, " I guarantee that sonuvabitch would 'go' if I was up there!" Be careful what you wish for!

The plane landed. Fred approached. "Why don't you take the guy up?" All eyes focused on me. I was caught between a rock and a hard place.

I took Rick aside and reviewed procedures including the danger of climbing in and out of the plane. He not only signed an affidavit that promised he would jump, he gave me his word!

A few minutes later we were airborne and at jump altitude. The plane started jump run. I told Rick that it was OK if he didn't want to jump, but if he got outside of the plane, he wasn't getting back in. He nodded agreement.

On command, Rick climbed out. I was confident this would be a textbook jump. We hit the exit point. I smacked Rick on the backside, pointed and yelled, "Go!" Nothing happened.

I did it again. Nothing happened.

The third time, he turned, looked at me and shook his head "no!"

He'd lied to me! He'd broken his word! I was incensed. I exploded. I reached out and tried to ply his fingers loose, to no avail. I pounded on his hands but he had wrapped his arms around the strut and was holding on for dear life. I grabbed the pilot's seat for leverage and shot out a right side kick catching him in the mid-section. He folded like a cheap card table and dropped away from the plane. I turned back to the other students; their eyes were as big as saucers. I'd done the right thing, but my conscience bothered me as I watched him drift into the trees a mile away.

By the time we landed, I was so guilt-ridden that I decided I'd let him take one complimentary swing at me, but no more!

Battered and bruised he huffed and puffed his way across the corn fields back to the drop zone. I prepared myself. He rushed up and threw his arms around me in a bone-crushing bear hug. Suddenly he started sobbing uncontrollably. As he pulled his head away he mouthed the words, "Thank you, thank you, thank you." All he needed was a little push.

Like Rick, many in this business want success but lack confidence. They need a push. If they're afraid to show the plan, hand them the marker a few seconds before the opportunity presentation begins and tell them that they're "up!" If they're afraid of the phone, hand it to them when you're talking to a prospect and say, "Tell them what you've found." If they are afraid of public speaking, call on them unexpectedly during a public presentation to talk about a product that excites them.

I promise, that if you do this, they'll throw their arms around you and say, "Thank you, thank you, thank you!"

# 13

# Prejudice

*Be a Victim or Accept Accountability for your own Success.*

**It was the late 60's. I'd busted my butt, completed four years of college in two and graduated Cum Laude.** I was Honorably Discharged from the military and had been wounded in action. I was married and had a child. I'd demonstrated intelligence, tenacity, stability and a willingness to accept responsibility, all of the qualifications necessary to snag a first class position with a premier company. I interviewed with over 50 corporations. Most never called back. The few that did, offered condolences. I didn't understand it?

On my 54$^{th}$ interview I spoke at length with a recruiter for a billion dollar Oil Company. The interview went great! We discussed everything from my family life and military experience to my plans for the future. At the conclusion, the gentleman told me I was ineligible for the position. I asked "Why? I thought we got along famously?" He replied that he'd "be    honest" with me. There was an unwritten policy against hiring Vietnam veterans. The company couldn't a take a chance on hiring vets and having any of them "go off" and shoot somebody! I couldn't believe it!

"Why'd you spend four hours with me if you knew I was unhireable?" He said he'd been a navigator on a B24 in WWII and could relate to me. He'd had a family when he got out of the service. He said I was exactly what he was looking for but he couldn't consider veterans. After that I hid my veteran status and had more job offers than I could handle.

At one point, I taught in the inner city. I'd enjoyed it and planned on staying, however it became apparent that it was a dead end career choice. Perhaps to compensate for past inequities, 100% of the promotions went to African-Americans, whether they were competent or not.

In my late twenties I applied to medical school. I was well qualified. In Vietnam I'd delivered babies, pulled teeth and treated trauma. I'd spent several years in pharmaceuticals and had experience in the emergency room and the operating room. I worked at several medical teaching institutions and also taught a course at N.I.H. for which physicians received graduate credit. I was well respected in the medical community. I had a truckload of references. While the Dean of Admissions agreed that I was well qualified, he told me that I was "the wrong age, the wrong sex and the wrong color." I didn't get in. The normal attrition rate was two dropouts in fours years. The class that I applied for lost sixteen in the freshman year!

My brother and I went through the process for a small business loan. We were both Purple Heart veterans. In spite of sailing through the loan process we were ultimately told all loan guarantees were going to minorities.

In spite of an equal rights law in my state, 25 years ago gaining child custody was a nightmare for men. The courts had a rubber stamp that said, "Mothers Only!" even if the moms were proven grossly incompetent. I was fortunate.

When my daughter was ten, she wanted to join the Girl scouts but was told they wouldn't accept any girl whose parent didn't participate. Naturally, I went to the meeting to sign up. I was informed fathers weren't allowed. Because I was a single Dad, my daughter was denied access to the troop. The Girl Scout Leader told me that I posed a potential danger to little girls.

I could write a book on the inequities that I've experienced. Folks who are black, brown, yellow or red don't own the corner on discrimination. Is there intolerance? Sure. Is there a glass ceiling? Maybe. But it all evens out. Ultimately, it's about accepting personal accountability rather than having someone provide you with a guaranteed meal ticket. Coming from a lower, middle class background, I sure didn't have a leg up on anybody else. Whatever prejudice I experienced only made me stronger and more determined to succeed.

A capitalistic society is about making money. Any management with two brain cells is going to hire the best person for the job, regardless of ethnicity. If they don't, their competition will. If they're too stupid to hire the best person, why would you want to work for them anyway? Forget taking them to court, if you really want revenge, go to work for their competition or better yet, go to work for yourself. Living well is the best revenge.

Network marketing is capitalism at its finest. If you work hard and smart, and come from an attitude of success, sooner or later you'll make it. You can become a professional victim and sit around feeling sorry for yourself or you can make the decision to be the master of your own destiny. Be proactive. Let discrimination become a motivating force.

You've been given the vehicle. The rest is up to you!

# 14

# Getting a Haircut

*It's about commitment!*

**I couldn't have been prouder of my son.** He finally got a haircut! Yeah!!! Got a haircut? Why should I have been proud of him for that? Do I judge him by the length of his hair? Why hadn't I just marched him to the barbershop as my father had done with me?

First of all, he was 29 years old. Old enough to make his own decisions about his hair or anything else he wants to do in life. Secondly, I didn't judge him by the length of his hair but by the purity of his heart. For that he got an A+. But, and it's a big but, people invariably make first impression decisions based on appearance. Maybe it shouldn't be that way, but it is.

You see he's a network marketer and, at that point in time, he wasn't making the money that allowed him the liberty to be unconventional (eccentric if you're wealthy). At one time, he was earning serious money but he had gotten away from doing the business. His lifestyle changed. He'd grown his hair long, real long! The ladies not only loved it, they envied it. Eventually, his income faltered but he had fallen into a groove. We all do. It's called our comfort zone. That's why some people work the 45-year plan.

He'd lost sight of the fact that to attract folks into this business, you have to represent what *their* idea of a successful business man or women looks and acts like. Most folks associate success with a traditional appearance. Whether that's right or wrong is irrelevant.

The real point is not the length of his hair but the strength of his commitment. He had gotten back into attending and holding meetings and trainings nearly every day of the week. He was moving retail product and inviting folks to look at the plan but he was wearing a badge of non-conformity that was hurting him. He was involved, not committed. Getting his hair cut was the missing piece in his willingness to do whatever it takes to be successful. Gradually he came back to the realization that success is always commensurate with commitment and that folks follow committed people. Now that his commitment is complete, he is on his way to being the architect of his destiny.

The price for success is paid upfront. That price is different for everyone but everyone who becomes successful pays the price. For him it was surrendering his personal right to choose his own appearance. For others maybe it's making a greater time commitment when they are already working two jobs. Maybe it's talking to more people even if they're incredibly shy. Former business managers with M.B.A.s may have to put their egos in their back pockets and follow the direction of a high school drop out who has become a successful network marketer. Sales people have to unlearn the art of building a case and learn to dispense information rather than convince.

Commitment always involves giving up something——Happy Hour, bowling, hunting, fishing, and time at the gym... My sponsors unplugged their TV for a year; I had two folks sell their homes and move into apartments. I know of folks who have cancelled family vacations. My wife Gingie and I completely cleared our calendars and either attended or held a meeting every day for three years. We listened to cassette tapes every day. We used every product and talked to everyone who came into contact with us. I gave up martial arts and my long time dream of becoming a Master, a 4th degree black belt. Our families thought we were nuts. Years later they're still working and we're financially independent. Was it worth it to be committed? You bet! We weren't balanced but we were certainly focused. We made the commitment, put the blinders on and turned on the laser beam. Thank God! When my health unexpectedly went south, we were debt free and on solid financial ground.

Ironically some local distributors told my son that he was foolish to surrender his identity. I couldn't help but wonder if subconsciously they were unnerved because they saw that he had made a total commitment to give up something important to him to attain success-to do what he doesn't want to do today so that he can do what he wants to do tomorrow. It's not about the length of his hair; it's about his future. His action put them on notice. It has caused them to question their own commitment. What were they willing to give up to take it to the next level?

Finally, my son has in his toolbox one of the most powerful tools in network marketing-the right to not only ask but also to expect others who claim that they want to be successful to match their commitment to his. The neat thing is that once he has attained the level that he wants, he can wear his hair to the floor and get away with it!

Earnings are a barometer of your leadership. Your leadership is a barometer of your commitment. Show me any business or organization that is not maximizing success and I'll show you management that is not committed.

Jim Ridinger, the founder of the "Unfranchise System" that has blossomed into a nine figure direct sales company, says it best: "Those who succeed do what those who fail are unwilling to do."

# 15

# Setting the Standard

*Teaching in the County.*

**In spite of horror tales about teaching inner city kids, I loved it**. The kids were responsive to positive reinforcement and generally eager to learn. Unfortunately for me, promotions were mandated to reflect the changing demographics of the student population. Teaching in the city was a dead end career choice. I transferred to the suburbs.

My assignment was 12th grade in a blue-collar section of the county. Not surprising, as a new guy, I was assigned kids who were labeled under achievers or disciplinary problems. No sweat! I accepted responsibility for kids who couldn't have cared less about learning.

In spite of rampant absenteeism and poor academic performance, there was intense political pressure for social promotions. The system was a joke. The County Government intimidated the Board of Education, which intimidated the administration, which intimidated the faculty, who went along with the program. There was no accountability except passing grades. I was there to do a job. I didn't sign on to be a babysitter!

I recorded more failing grades than any teacher in school. I believed teachers were abrogating their responsibility if they didn't have at least 20% failures! Sound harsh? Do the math. At least six out of every class (of thirty) never showed up.

The standards were so low that students who passed everything through the tenth grade could graduate providing they had English credits for the 11th and 12th grade and passed U.S. History. If, by senior year, students were lacking the necessary credits to graduate, pressure was put on the 12th grade teachers to pass them. I had one student, in the twelfth grade, whose literacy only extended to writing his own name! That sickened me.

I set the standard for performance and conduct the first day of school. Class was non-stop work from the minute they entered the room until they left. I gave tests, drills, and homework every day. Not much homework, but enough to build good habits. The kids hated me with a passion. They wanted to know why I didn't "rap" with them like other teachers. One day I went into my room and in big letters scrawled across the blackboard was "Mr. Keefer's P.O.W. Camp!"

I had a standard for respect. Early on, one student challenged me in front of the class. He was a monster who played on the football team and had a reputation as a bully. I asked him to join me in the hall where I stood toe-to toe and eyeball to chin, looking up at him. "Are you inviting me to knock that chip off your shoulder?" I whispered. He got the message. I'd learned in the military and while teaching in city schools that once you earned the respect of the tough guys, there'd be no discipline problems with others.

Although neither my demeanor as a disciplinarian nor my performance standards ever wavered, by the time the first semester was closing out, kids were cutting other classes to sit in my room. The time went fast, they learned something and they felt good about themselves. At Christmas I'd get more gifts than any other teacher in school.

In spite of my apparent effectiveness, every June I was called into the principle's office to justify my grades. On one occasion, I sat in the principle's office with a kid who wasn't going to graduate. The principle looked at the kid and said, "Tell me, how Mr. Keefer failed to meet your individual needs and differences?" The kid said, "Excuse me?" The question was repeated verbatim. The student looked at the principle and said, " I don't know what you're talking about?" The principal said, "Why'd you fail?"

The kid responded, "I didn't do any work!" It was perfect!

I was questioned about another student. The principle asked, "Why'd this kid fail?" I responded, "He only showed up 15 days the whole year!" The principle asked. "What was the quality of his work those 15 days?" I said, "Who cares? Would you pay me for the whole year if I only showed up 15 days?" He told me I had an attitude problem. I was still unwilling to compromise. He passed the kid anyway. The next year, I was transferred to the 7th grade.

Ironically, The Senior Class voted me runner up for Best Teacher of the Year every year I was there. I asked the kids why they voted for a tough taskmaster like me? The response was, "You made us do stuff."

I also established standards in my network marketing business and stuck by them. I presented prospects with a list of requirements: three way calling, voice mail, attendance at seminars, auto ship, retail customers, etc. If they balked, they could find another sponsor. If I decided to bring them on board I expected them to "do stuff." I held them accountable. I expected them to duplicate my system. What I set in motion carried in motion. In my first full year, I had a half dozen distributors hit a quarter million dollars annualized.

# 16

# Leadership Styles

*Control vs. Empowerment*

**I listened today as the pundits evaluated the President Elect's intelligence and speculated on his leadership ability.** By most accounts, he was rated as an intellectual lightweight, incapable of handling the job. Conversely, his former challenger was cast as a scholar, much more academically attuned to addressing the toughest job in the world.

Ironically, none mentioned that the President Elect is a graduate of both Yale and Harvard, where he earned an M.B.A. He is the first president to earn a graduate business degree. Nor was it mentioned that as a military officer, he flew jet fighters; none of these accomplishments a task for dummies. Nor did they mention that his opponent, posting mostly 'Cs' and Ds, had a less spectacular undergraduate record, that he was kicked out of graduate school after failing five of eight courses or that as a result of mediocre grades, he dropped out of law school. The commentary prompted me to reflect on the qualities needed for leadership.

I have been fascinated with leadership since I met Danny Doherty when I was ten years old. He was two years older. His charisma was mesmerizing. In the scouts he was the patrol leader. He displayed patience with his younger charges and he led by example. Danny, more than being "the boss," was a teacher, a youthful Yoda. It is only within recent years that I have realized the indelible influence this 12-year-old mentor had on my own approach to leadership.

In high school, as the 17-year-old president of a fraternity, I was charged with handling the administrative and financial duties of maintaining the fraternity house. I learned that besides being a mentor, there were responsibilities associated with leadership.

A few years later in the Marine Corps, I learned about the delegation of authority. I learned that fundamental to being a good leader, one had to be a good follower and duplicate the process. I learned the duty of the leader to develop teamwork and serve those in your charge.

Discipline, personal accountability and self-confidence are instrumental to these skills. In that pre-Vietnam era these concepts were harshly taught in Boot Camp through fear, physical intimidation and negative reinforcement. Although these techniques are illegal today, they produced magnificent results. Those lessons instilled a drive to accomplish the mission, and an appreciation for teamwork and tiers of leadership. My later service reinforced no matter how good a leader was, the success of the mission depended on the effectiveness of successive junior leaders.

For almost 50 years I've been a serious student of leadership. Credentialed with nearly two decades each in the military and corporate America and over a decade in network marketing, I've concluded that leadership is a science. All styles can be reduced to two basic approaches: autocratic control and delegated management.

Clearly the most prevalent management style is autocratic control. People want to be "in charge." The leader sees himself (or herself) as omniscient and surrounds himself with folks that can be molded to his philosophy. He wants people to listen to him. He wants to create dedicated followers who won't question him. He fears loss of control will usurp his plan. He doesn't trust the intellect or motives of subordinates. He believes that the most effective method of control is intimidation and fear of loss. His decisions are based solely on his previous experiences or self-interests.

As business grows he frequently gets bogged down involving himself with minutia and the growth pains that are a result of the failure of his management style. His demise usually results in the collapse of the organization. Ultimately, the full potential for success is never realized.

The delegated management approach is more complex and much riskier but the ultimate rewards are greater. This system magnifies the insecurity of the autocrat because it appears to involve the surrender of control. The proponent surrounds himself with individuals of equal or greater competence and benchmarks his experience against theirs. He entrusts them with responsibility and decision-making authority. He believes that power is not lost, but gained, by giving it away. He believes that delegated authority breeds personal accountability and creates co-ownership in the mission.

This system is designed to fine tune leaders in lieu of going through the arduous process of building them from scratch. Because there is a legitimate infrastructure in place, the demise of the leader will have little impact on continuation of the mission.

Neither system is a democracy, but in this system the leader acts decisively, but only acts when absolutely necessary. All problems are handled at the lowest level possible to resolve the situation. Contrary to the autocratic control management style where the leader insists on having his (or her) finger on everything that happens (usually as a result of lack of confidence in subordinates to effectively manage on their own), in the delegated management style, there should rarely, if ever, be an internal situation that reaches upper level executive management.

The confidence displayed by the delegated management style builds the self-esteem and confidence of junior leaders. This system is not however an apprenticeship to develop leaders. The mission is far too important. In this system, the very best people are put in place up front and fine-tuned, not created.

Autocrats incorrectly believe that money is the key to motivation. They fail to realize that money doesn't inspire loyalty to the mission, only to money. Participation in a common cause inspires loyalty. My experience as a military advisor to various indigenous peoples around the world substantiates that the unit effectiveness of the emotionally committed supercedes that of "professional" mercenaries. Lack of inclusion in being part of the solution, not money, is what precipitates successful earners to leave their respective companies to contribute elsewhere.

Why deal with the aggravation of handling all of the problems yourself? Find good people, include them in the process, and with a little monitoring, you can sit back, relax and enjoy the show.

# 17

# The Ballad of the Black Beret

*Free has no value!*

**Beginning June 2001, the US Army will issue black berets to all new recruits as part of their basic uniform.**

Around the globe, the beret has traditionally been reserved for the elite—paratroops and other highly motivated volunteers who successfully complete incredibly challenging commando-type qualification courses.

Born of esprit de corps, the special breed that earns the right to wear the beret accept the fact that during hostilities they will be part of the 10% who spearhead the fighting, virtually assuring them of being killed or wounded.

There is also significance and international tradition to the color of the beret.

Worldwide, the airborne, who serve as shock troops, wear red or maroon.

Special Forces have become known by the color of their distinctive headgear, the Green Beret. Their primary mission is behind enemy lines, training indigenous troops.

Because of the grueling and unbelievably rigorous selection process, the Black Beret worn by the US Army Airborne Ranger, the American commando, is arguably the most prestigious of all berets. This is the beret that the army is now giving away.

Because our numbers are small, the public is mostly unfamiliar with the prestige of the Black Beret, although they may have seen it illegitimately worn by puss-gutted color guards of some veterans' organizations or scruffy unkempt wannabees in a flimsy attempt to enhance their own stature. The military bearing of a true Ranger however is unmistakable.

The process to become a Ranger starts with an in-depth background investigation and interview. I had nine years of military service, served as a Marine grunt, had led nearly 200 combat patrols and ambushes and was serving as a Special Forces "A" Team commander at the time of application. These qualifications were no more impressive than those of my fellow students, most of whom were professional soldiers.

At age 27, I needed a medical waiver, as did all of those over age 24. While stamina and conditioning are a major part of being a Ranger, Rangers are more than hairy-chested knuckle-draggers. The academic requirements are tougher than any college course that I've ever taken.

The Q-Course is a 3-4 month leadership evaluation program administered under the harshest conditions imaginable. I attended the particularly brutal winter program.

After being successfully evaluated in basic military skills the real leadership evaluation begins. Candidates are daily rotated in and out of leadership positions and graded on their command performance in all phases of combat operations: writing highly detailed operations orders, movement to the target and finally the assault and exfiltration.

Operating almost exclusively under cover of darkness and using a compass to navigate, candidates may spend hours paddling small boats over open seas or infiltrate at night by parachute but mostly they daily march dozens of miles to their targets traversing icy mountainous terrain or wading neck deep in frigid alligator and snake-infested swamps.

Confined to wet clothes, in freezing weather for weeks on end, with no rest between patrols and limited to only one meal a day, students become severely malnourished, suffer from sleep deprivation and hypothermia. Body temperatures plummet to 95F. Black and white troops alike turn blue and shiver uncontrollably. Even the strongest become incoherent and hallucinate. Using rope, troops attach themselves to their weapons, gear and fellow students lest they wander off or lose their equipment. Half-frozen, soaking wet and starving, many candidates are reduced to babbling idiots. With no end to their suffering in sight, and overwhelmed by the pressures of the mission, some lose the will to live, choosing instead to sit down in the swamps and freeze to death.

Those in leadership positions are evaluated on their ability to maintain discipline, tactical unit cohesion and a sense of mission under these extraordinary circumstances. No leadership challenge is more demanding.

Of the original 210 that started, only twenty of the thirty who survived earned enough points to graduate; 2 out of every 21.

At 210 lbs with a 31" waist, I was in the best shape of my life when I started the course. By graduation I had lost 65 pounds and spent three weeks in the hospital recuperating. But, I had paid the price to wear the coveted Black Beret that the Army is now giving away free.

What does all of this have to do with network marketing? Simply this:

Free has no value. The Army won't attract recruits for long by giving away the most prestigious of symbols. The Black Beret will become so commonplace that its value will be meaningless.

So too, will the value of your products if you sell them at cost or below full suggested retail, and so too will the opportunity if you beg or entice any prospect who can fog a mirror instead of utilizing a rigorous selection process to identify those with the commando-like tenacity necessary to become successful.

Remember, the higher the value that you place on your business the quicker candidates of quality will appear and the sooner you will earn the *Beret of Success*.

# 18

# Dreaming Big!

*Providence will reward you*

**William James, the noted British philosopher, said it best over a hundred years ago. "What the mind of man can believe, he can achieve."** "What one sets in motion, carries in motion." It's the universal law of nature.

It was verified again early this century. Andrew Carnegie, the eccentric Scottish capitalist, commissioned Napoleon Hill to study the 100 most successful people of his day to determine whether there was a common ingredient to their success. Over a period of twenty-five years, Hill conducted thousands of interviews with such diverse notables as Thomas Edison, the Wright Brothers, Wrigley and Henry Ford. The conclusion: they all knew where they were going. To a person, they had a written personal business plan. Today we call that written plan a goal statement.

Something magical happens when we decide to take charge of our lives and consummate a written contract with ourselves. Success is commensurate with commitment. A written contract with yourself is the foundation of that commitment.

A while back a successful network marketer from Charlotte, NC told me that years earlier he and his wife had sat down and planned their future in writing. Somehow, over time, that list of dreams and aspirations had been misplaced and forgotten. Seven years later while going through old papers the list appeared. They were dumbfounded. Seventy-five percent of their goals had been realized!

73

Materially, my goals have been very modest. Money or lack of it was never the issue. I've lived all over the world. I've enjoyed every adventure imaginable. I've lived the "lifestyle of the rich and famous" whether I had money or not.

So six years ago when I started my career with Market America, it was tough to develop a meaningful goal statement. Something must have gotten me dreaming because as I remember it, the conclusion of my written goal, was to retire on the water with my own pier and a boat.

I was moving steadfastly toward that goal when I was unexpectedly diagnosed with end stage heart disease. The prognosis was bleak at best. Living became my goal. I forgot about everything else. A year later I happened to be talking to a fellow distributor who knew of a contemporary three story structure on the water with a terrific panoramic view. It even had a little pier with the water just ten feet from the house. There was no maintenance. Gingie and I bought it. I hadn't seen my goal statement in years but surely this satisfied my dream. It was most likely my last home. I didn't realize that providence had other plans in store for me.

Three years later, two years ago, one of our dearest friends moved his lovely wife and four beautiful daughters from a cramped two-bedroom condo near Baltimore to the Eastern Shore of Maryland where he had built a dream home. While visiting him, we unexpectedly stumbled onto the home of our dreams, an old barn built in Princeton, NJ in 1820 and relocated on ten and a half acres of mature forest on a point that projected into the juncture of the beautiful and expansive Wye and East Wye Rivers. A hundred feet from the house a pier, big enough to moor a 60' motor yacht, bisected nearly a half-mile of water frontage. The property backed up to hundreds of acres mature forest that would never be developed. The land was home to countless deer and other wildlife including a pair of bald eagles. I couldn't believe the incredible feeling of belonging that both my wife and I intrinsically felt. It was made for us.

Several weeks later my son came across my long-forgotten goal statement. He immediately faxed me a copy. There in black and white was an exact description of our new home that could have been substituted verbatim for ad copy on the same Wye River Estate.

It was all there: the name of the place, the type of house, the surroundings, the location of the pier, the distance from the house to the pier, the serenity...the description was perfect in every detail. It sent chills up and down my spine.

Over the years, because of my health and other concerns, I had forgotten the vividness of our dream. But, six years earlier, that image had been burned into my brain by twice daily reading my goal statement. My subconscious had not forgotten and it had come to pass.

So when the modern sages of personal development tell you that goal statements are outdated and there are more scientific approaches to success, don't believe it. Just remember my story and the success stories of those giants interviewed by Napoleon Hill.

Dream big. Commit it to writing. Read it twice daily; better yet, rewrite it at least once a day. Come from a belief that it will happen and you will be the architect of your destiny.

# 19

# The Price of Pizza
*What are You Willing to Pay for Success?*

**Precedent to the unequivocal conviction that success is a foregone conclusion is the understanding that success is neither cheap nor gratis.** When I say that there are no free lunches, believe it! Every successful person pays the price and the price is relative to each individual.

Let's use pizza as an analogy. If you want a plain cheese pizza, it's six bucks. If you want a deluxe pizza with the works, it's fourteen bucks. While you might have a love affair with that toasty crust smothered with 16 different toppings and a plain pizza makes you gag, if you're unwilling to pay more than six dollars, guess what? You are only going to get the plain pizza! Life's the same way. You only get what you are willing to pay for.

But your case is different, right? You want to earn a hundred thousand dollars a year—-or maybe a million. You want to pay the price, but just can't. It's not your fault. You're heavily in debt and can't afford the tools necessary to build the business. You're already working two jobs and don't have the time. Your husband or wife thinks that you're an idiot for getting sucked into a "pyramid scheme." You're a professional and embarrassed to tell people that you're in "this" kind of business. You've already committed your evenings to the bowling team. You're physically disabled. You have health problems. You're afraid to speak in public. You fear rejection.

Welcome to the club!

Your price is no higher than anyone else's. You're just not willing to pay it. It's all relative. This business has a way of testing you in those areas where you are most vulnerable and subject to capitulate. You need to overcome that if you really want to be successful. You are the only one who can determine what you are willing to pay.

Remember too, you can't make payments once you're successful. The price for success is *always* paid up front.

In 1967, the year I was discharged from the military, the ticket to success was a college degree. I had barely squeaked through high school. My concern about my academic prowess was compounded by the unexpected animosity that I faced from both faculty and students alike as one of the first returning Vietnam veterans. I had seen life at its rawest and I wanted to become financially successful to insulate myself from as much misery as possible. College, in my mind, was the answer. I had to get that degree, but looking ahead to four years of abuse on campus was unimaginable. I made a decision to pay whatever price was necessary to get the degree as quickly as possible.

While my peers were cutting classes, drinking beer, smoking dope and enjoying "free love," I put the blinders on. I canceled my G.I. Bill and hid my veteran status. Driving a cab to support myself, I concurrently enrolled in three different colleges. I attended school both day and night, never missing a single class. I completed fours years of undergraduate work, including remedial courses, in two years and graduated Cum Laude, eleventh in my class. Sound impressive? Maybe it is, but I'm no Einstein. I just showed up. Others didn't. I was willing to pay the price. They weren't.

I learned from that experience. Don't half step through life. Play full out or don't play at all. Success is commensurate with the price you pay.

That willingness to pay the price was a standard that I set for myself over thirty years ago. It became a habit. It has provided the impetus in my drive towards success in all areas of my life. Have I had challenges along the way? You don't even want to know.

Fast forward to network marketing. On day one I made a commitment to pay the price. By the end of that first year I was at $300,000 annualized. No toys for me. All my earnings went for living expenses or back into the business. The second year I hit over a half million annualized. Same, same. I was going for freedom, not "stuff." By the end of the third year, I was debt free. I'd achieved my goal but I'd paid the price. . I hadn't taken a single day off for three years. Not one. Some days I showed the plan 6 or 7 times.

Was I balanced? Heck no! Was I focused? Like a laser beam! Was it worth it? You bet! I was working towards freedom and having fun at the same time. For the first time in years I felt no job stress.

After the start of my fourth year I became critically ill. I was diagnosed with terminal heart disease, most likely a result of some virus that I picked up in a third world country. But my family's financial future was secure. In the process other families became debt-free. You see my goal was not just for myself, but also for others. I wanted the best retention rate and the highest number of legitimate big money earners, not front-end loaders, in the industry. I achieved that. My personally sponsored people who followed the plan and who were willing to pay the price, without exception, duplicated my success.

May I take your order? Plain pizza or deluxe?

# Tracking vs. Prospecting

*The Art of Spotting Opportunity.*

**Every schoolboy fantasizes about living on the wild frontier**-or at least they did when I was a kid. TV was in its infancy and, with the exception of a Saturday afternoon matinee, most of our vicarious experiences were stimulated through books or the radio. Imaginations ran wild while reading stories of Jim Bridger, John Coulter and Lewis and Clark. Then came the Davy Crockett craze. Young boys envisioned themselves tracking (wild Indians) and stalking (game). To kids nowadays, tracking means correcting the play of their VCR and stalking is a crime against women. The world has changed.

I was five years old when we moved from the country to the city. In those days there were no suburbs. Where the concrete stopped, the farms began. Where I lived there was a buffer of about twenty acres between the two. It was known as "The Bird Sanctuary." At age eight or nine I would leave the asphalt and steal away into the woods. I would journey down the stream looking for animal tracks. I could identify the footprints of raccoon, opossum, squirrel, rat and rabbit. I learned to track the animals to their dens and burrows. I made plaster casts of their tracks. It was an exciting time.

My tracking skills became more finely tuned a few years later as a Boy Scout. I could now estimate the age of tracks by the sharpness of their imprint. I could recognize disturbance to vegetation.

In the Marine Corps, instructors created "enemy" trails using outdated human blood from local hospitals. We were taught how to follow those trails and determine their age and the nature, severity and type of wound by the color and composition of the blood. We learned the significance of the stool in determining the age of "sign" and the health of the prey. We learned to identify a man or woman, and sometimes their age, by urine patterns. In land mine warfare school I learned that the Viet Cong marked their mines, but the markings were subtle and hard to see unless one was extremely observant of the environment. On at least one occasion this skill saved my life.

A few years later, as an Army Ranger, I attended "graduate level" courses on tracking. I learned the importance of ground color in determining the age of tracks and that color is dependent upon temperature, humidity, time of day and season. I learned to more acutely evaluate damage to spider webs, grass and foliage. I became more astute at reading the mind of the quarry and thinking like them to determine their course of action.

My skills came into play in the Special Forces (Green Beret) where I was sometimes called upon to teach classes on escape, evasion and survival and how to avoid leaving a trail for the enemy to follow.

Then came a period of my life when I was financially destitute. For over a year I relied on field skills and experience in the bush to put meat on the table. But, except for combat, nowhere have my skills been more tested than hunting Big Game in Africa. Like in combat, a mistake can be fatal. The hunter may become the hunted. Wounded or stalked game, like enemy soldiers, often circle around behind the hunter and ambush him. It happens quickly. There is little time to respond. Additionally, there is always a danger of being stalked by hungry predatory animals, hostile natives or guerrilla soldiers of some internal political faction. There is also the very real risk of being bitten by highly venomous snakes or insects. As in war, attention must be focused not only on the tracks in front of you, but also on what's going on around you.

I've been in the African bush over a dozen times. On most occasions I've had the privilege to observe the tracking skills of native Bushmen. Small in physical stature, these amazing tribesmen are a simple and peaceful people. Unfortunately they have been all but wiped out by tribal warfare over the years. As they move into the 21st century, their skills, no longer needed for survival, are being lost. But the proficiency of the few who have retained the old ways is mesmerizing.

I've watched them utilize the senses: sight, smell, hearing and intuition (and to a lesser degree, touch and taste) in the relentless pursuit of their quarry. With the naked eye they see things at a thousand yards that I can't see with binoculars. They see almost imperceptible spoor at three feet that I don't see until it is pointed out.

I understand basic movement patterns (humans and big game take the same evasive zig zag action to mislead predators), but their acute knowledge of movement patterns specific to each animal is incredible.

If they lose the trail, they'll gather together in conference. Sitting on their haunches, in barely audible terms, they softly communicate in Fana Galo (an amalgamation of the five basic African dialects and Afrikaans). Their business-like conversations are punctuated with numerous gestures and an occasional "hmmm which indicates acknowledgement rather than agreement. Then these masters of the bush are off again.

Prospecting is much like tracking. In both cases you are looking for an elusive prey. In both cases you need to understand the thought processes of your quarry. And, in both cases you need to utilize your senses and be observant to what's happening. Unlike traditional tracking, you don't need years of practice or inherited intuition to spot "sign". The quarry will present itself to you. The most important skill required is your sense of hearing. You need to educate yourself to listen to what is being said by each and every person that you come in contact with. Once you become skilled at listening, you will find that 100% of the folks that you engage in conversation are targets. They will present themselves for a "clean shot." They'll bring up the business. All you have to be able to do is pick up "sign." What is "sign"? In network marketing it's a complaint. That complaint will be about something in their lives related to the lack of time or money.

Doubt what I'm saying? To learn to pick up "sign," start carrying a small pocket notebook and, after the fact, document the first few minutes of your conversations with others. You will find that almost the first words out of everyone's mouths are complaints. This is an opportunity to "shoot," but because you are not used to listening, at first you'll miss this "sign." You may even forget to jot down the conversation to validate what I'm saying. Once you see that notebook in your pocket however, you'll remember why it's there. Shortly thereafter, you'll begin to develop the habit of keeping your diary. As you become more diligent about this process, you'll become aware that *every* conversation provides you with an opening to respond with the business. Soon, you'll begin to recognize these opportunities as they are happening, rather than after the fact. This usually takes about twenty times of logging conversations. "Oh yeah, Bob complained that he was working too much overtime." "Louise said she needed new living room furniture." Do you get the message?

You've read "sign". You've got the quarry in your crosshairs. Your business opportunity is the magic bullet that will bag your prey. Your killing shot is the solution to their time and money problem. Now comes the tricky part, "squeezing off the shot." You must be able to pull the trigger and score a clean hit. If you miss, you'll scare away your prey. He or she will become wary and, like the impala or the whitetail deer, bolt the next time they see you. Most likely, you'll never get another shot.

How do you score that hit without saying the wrong thing? That critical subject is covered in two chapters, **Big Game Hunting**, *Bagging the Heavy Hitter* and **Small Game Hunting**, *The Stability of Your Organization* in Volume Two, entitled **Continuing the Journey**.

In the mean time, purchase that pocket notebook and begin logging those complaints until you learn to pick them up in real time. When you can do that subconsciously, you'll be ready to learn how to shoot.

# 21

# The Alaskan Pipeline

*Success is not an overnight phenomenon.*

**It was the early 80's. The cold war was hot. Terrorism was a global concern.** As a principle in an international security company, I was in the right place at the right time.

Our cadre was composed of former special operations types with combat and law enforcement experience. We trained foreign military units and Special Weapons And Tactics teams for police on four continents. Central to our mission was profiling the security of nuclear power plants and other high-risk facilities critical to national interests. We were authorized by Congress to evaluate the security of the Alaskan Pipeline.

Traveling the 1100 miles from Valdez in the south, to Prudhoe Bay in the north, and seeing the full expanse of the Alaskan wilderness firsthand was one of the richest experiences of my life. In the south, the abundant forests and mountains were breath-taking and magnificent. The temperature was cold, but exhilarating. A thousand miles to the north, 250 miles above the Arctic Circle, the topography was bleak and foreboding. There was ice-covered tundra as far as the eye could see. It was brutally cold.

When I arrived at Dead Horse, at the top of the world, the temperature was 65°F below zero excluding the wind chill index. Twenty seconds after leaving the plane (the engines were kept running to keep them from freezing) the cold kicked me in the face with the force of a mule. I was terrified that my face would suddenly be flash frozen. The fact that man had built facilities and could live in this hostile environment was an incredible tribute to human ingenuity.

I saw firsthand the inconceivable pains that Alyeska, the conglomerate of oil companies, had taken to protect the environment, even in this most desolate region on earth. I saw none of the reckless disregard for our natural resources as reported by the media.

During the winter, we experienced several weeks of total darkness. Then the season changed slowly, minute-by-minute. In the beginning, by midday, we were blessed with a few seconds of twilight. Then a minute, then two minutes, then three….

It took weeks for full daylight to arrive; even then, it was only for a few hours daily. I remember sitting in a hotel dining room in Anchorage eating lunch, watching the sun come up at 2 PM only to set again by 4 PM.

When we weren't instructing the security force and conditions permitted, we flew nape of the earth visually inspecting the pipeline. In the twilight, even cities the size of Fairbanks took on the aura of ghost towns. We watched moose the size of minivans lazily ambling through deserted streets as though they were the only creatures on earth.

The Chief of Security was genetically acclimated to the harshness of the North. His family had settled the Alaskan frontier generations earlier. As the former Superintendent of the State Police, with responsibility for a landmass two and a half times the size of Texas, he was accustomed to the challenges of climate and geography.

His Assistant, a former federal agent, was totally out of his element. He had been recruited from the hot, muggy bayous of the Mississippi Delta.

One evening I asked his wife how her family had handled the incredible transition from the Deep South to the Frigid North. She had wanted no part of it, but her husband was adamant. Begrudgingly, she packed up the kids and followed. Once there, a pioneer spirit awakened in her. She began a love affair with our 49th state.

She spoke passionately about the magnificence of Alaska, the change in lifestyle and the adjustments she had made. She explained that during the winter months people, like animals, nearly went into a state of hibernation. Life became dormant. Cabin fever could cause depression, but there was a bonding among the populace. They were content in accepting that in time, as she always did, spring would raise her yawning head. And what a glorious awakening it would be, as life burst forth in a magnitude greater than anything imaginable.

The days became longer until the land enjoyed 24 hours of light. Temperatures warmed. Flowers and vegetables grew to humungous sizes. Spirits became euphoric. Kids played outside until well after midnight. Sleep was no longer as necessary as their bodies adjusted accordingly. She became part of the great mystique.

Her discourse reminded me of so many of Aesop's Fables, the tortoise and the hare, the ant and the grasshopper and others. It reminded me of the cyclical nature of network marketing.

Achievement in this business is usually not an overnight phenomenon. Often we must endure a long cold winter before the buds of success begin to show. As they blossom, so too does our appreciation for the growth phase and the satisfaction that comes from enduring the dormancy that is part of the journey.

Her story regarding the changing of seasons reminds us of the peaks and valleys of life. We must prepare for the winter with the confidence of knowing that spring will surely come again.

Enjoy the bonding of those who make the journey with you and you'll surely share with them the euphoria of success.

# 22

# If They Don't Listen

*Why would you steer them wrong?*

**I was awakened by the sound of incoming mortars.** The time: the late 1980's. The place: Central America. Combat in Nicaragua and El Salvador was raging. This was not my first trip to this war-torn region. I had previously served as a civilian military advisor to an anti-terrorist commando unit.

As a nation, we were still emasculated from our cop-out in Vietnam. Many of our politicians subscribed to the philosophy of creating any excuse necessary to prevent us from accepting international responsibility. The Boland Amendment shackled our capability to legally respond. As a civilian, I was not hamstrung by the constraints put on the American military. I worked in forward areas, off limits to U.S. military personnel. Whether the politicians understood it or not, it was clearly in the interest of our own national security to preempt the spread of hostilities before they crossed the border into the Southern U.S. I was committed to play my part.

Anyone who doubted the intent of a Cuban led insurgency to overthrow the region and gain a toehold in the U.S., only had to see the enormous stockpile of munitions captured in the Grenada invasion in 1982.

Our liberal press was hoodwinking the American public by discrediting the validity of our involvement. Investigative journalism was almost non-existent. It was a common practice for reporters, enjoying the plush comforts of the Camino Real Hotel in Central America, to invite insurgent leaders to dine with them and then buy information from them. Typically, the information provided was nothing more than communist propaganda. Stories about the will of the people being usurped by the government were pablum. Stories about the atrocities attributed to right wing government forces in El Salvador were, for the most part, fabrications. These reporters would write anything to grab a bigger byline. I'd seen this type of self-serving journalism in Southeast Asia.

On rare trips to the capitol, I made it a practice to invite these journalists to come back with me to the hinterland to see what was really going on. Fearful to put their lives at risk, they'd weasel out. I'd then do my best to humiliate and discredit them in front of their peers.

In the hinterland——Indian country we called it, and it really was——the people were pro-American. Roving Cuban-led guerrilla forces would enter the villages and towns, kidnap their young men and press them into military service. Resistance meant immediate execution. Sometimes, for the family as well. These folks needed assistance.

We didn't have to worry about another Vietnam. They'd do their own fighting. What they needed was beans, bullets and bandages, and maybe a little military expertise. Their weapons were pathetic and barely functional. Medically, they had few supplies. Battle dressings were Kotex pads cut in half. Their wounded lay two to a bed. There was little, if any, anesthesia or antibiotics. Yet, their spirit was the best that I'd ever seen anywhere in the world.

My family has a legacy of military service that has been recognized by President Richard Nixon and Senators Bob Dole and John McCain. Growing up, it was a given for my brother and me, that someday we would be killed or wounded in battle.

92

After having seen the horror of combat, I was terrified that my kids would feel compelled to continue that legacy. I discouraged military service almost from the moment of birth.

However, I thought a small taste of real military service would enhance the boys' appreciation of life and the blessings of being an American. I envisioned that it would also be a great bonding experience for the three of us. I invited them to go with me to Central America. Frank opted to attend his high school graduation. Richard went.

Richard had beaten leukemia. I knew, more than his mother did, that he was of stout heart. But, he'd spent too many years tied to her apron strings. Those strings needed to be cut.

As a prelude to El Salvador, Richard needed to be shocked into reality of the situation. We went to Guatemala first. I put him through Guatemalan Airborne School. I ran his butt ragged. He performed magnificently. I was so proud of him. Then, on to El Salvador.

We were stationed and jumped with tough paracadistas (paratroops), but he fit right in. The days passed quickly. Soon, it was time to return home. I breathed a huge sigh of relief. We'd both come through our adventure unscathed. It was our last night in country. We would fly out of Illoponga the next day. I attempted to call his Mom and tell her that we were OK, but the guerrillas had blown up the telecommunications facility.

We turned in for the night. The incoming explosions shattered my sleep. I awoke and immediately looked for Richard. He was gone! I couldn't find him anywhere. I was terrified. I couldn't go home and tell his mother I'd gotten him killed. Maybe he'd jumped in a foxhole? The shelling stopped.

I frantically searched for hours. Shortly before dawn, he showed up, slightly tipsy with a smile on his face. He'd gone into town with a couple of young officers about his own age. They went looking for a couple of senoritas. I went ballistic. I couldn't believe that he was so stupid. I could have killed him.

"I was with Jose and Jos-B (I can't remember their names). I knew that I'd be OK."

"Why didn't you ask me?" I said.

"Because you wouldn't have let me go." He replied.

He was right about that. I was aware of dangers that he didn't understand. He felt insulted that I questioned him and he was becoming testy. I said, "You're my son. I love you."

Then I put him on the spot. I emphatically demanded that he "Give me one good reason why I wouldn't tell you exactly what you need to do to stay alive!"

I pressed the issue. He couldn't come up with an answer. I knew then that he gotten the message. I turned around and walked away. Once out of earshot, I burst into tears.

Have you ever had an analogous experience in network marketing? You bet. It may not have been life threatening, but the scenario is the same.

You're experienced in the business, like I was in a combat environment. Enter Nick (or Nancy) New Guy. You give him the blueprint for success. He goes off and follows his own program, just like Richard did.

When he shows up the next time you ask him why he's operating under his own agenda. You're aware of pitfalls and dangers that he doesn't understand. He feels insulted and becomes testy. No amount of logic will get through to him. Telling him he's uncoachable goes in one ear and out the other. How do you get him on the right track?

Remind him "My income is dependent upon your financial success." Then, put him on the spot. Emphatically demand that he give you one good reason why you wouldn't tell him exactly what he needed to do to succeed. Press the issue.

Worded and presented with the right posture, he won't be able to come up with an answer. You'll know then, that he got the message.

This is the only response, short of intimidating him by bringing in new blood, that I've found that has any chance of working with those who are uncoachable.

# 23

# Ethnic Pride

*Guinea, Kraut, the Chief, Fat Sweaty Wally....*
*A bigot's list of ethnic slurs? Not hardly!*

**I recently came across some old Christmas cards.** As I shuffled through the cards I realized how things have changed over the past 30 or 40 years. The names, as signed, would never pass muster today in an age where political correctness has undermined ethnic pride and replaced it with a victim mentality.

Thirty or forty years, sounds like an eternity! But, it seems only yesterday that *"the Kraut"* and I were donning military parachute gear for a night blast into some godforsaken, bug-infested no man's land. *"The Kraut"*, as he called himself, was a German immigrant who had joined the U.S. Army to become an American citizen. *"The Kraut"* distinguished himself by earning a direct commission for combat leadership in Vietnam.

Perhaps it was only last month, and not 1965, that *"the Chief"* and I sneaked into an off limits ARVN (Army of Vietnam) club only to barely escape with our lives a short time later after we had consumed too much firewater. *"The Chief"* was the son of an American Indian, an Osage warrior. His Dad had served proudly in WWII, Korea and Vietnam,

In those bygone days it was customary for people to be known by their ethnicity or appearance. Those names were worn with pride. So ingrained were the nicknames of yore that I never knew the first names of most of those folks who send us cards.

I do know that "*the Chief's*" first name is Jim. How bland when compared to a handle that stirs the imagination and conjures up images of fierce, half naked warriors bedecked in war bonnets kicking up huge dust trails riding their painted ponies across the plains.

At military and police department functions "*the Chief,*" like his ancestors, adorns his headgear with two miniature feathers, one symbolizing that he was wounded in battle, the other that he defeated an enemy warrior in mortal combat. To strip "*the Chief*", now a retired police officer, of his adopted nickname and call him just plain "Jim" would steal the identity that had earned him his department's highest award for valor. But were I to call him "*Chief*" publicly, undoubtedly someone within earshot would come to his defense and thrash me unmercilessly for my "insensitivity".

Then there was "*Guinea;*" "*Guinea the Lover*" was the way he preferred to be addressed. An Italian from New York, he would tell you in no uncertain terms which nationality had the corner on romantic men. On liberty "*Guinea*" dressed like a pimp and wore women's fragrances ("the ladies feel more comfortable and less threatened"). He was oblivious to remarks that kidded him about his masculinity. He always left the base with a smile but returned with a grin. What can I say?

"*F.S.W...Fat, Sweaty Wally*", is a retired steel worker. He was one of the first advisors to the South Vietnamese Popular Forces. How he came by his nickname I'll never know. Today he is understatedly portly. In those days, infantry types were hardly overweight. At the very most, he may have carried an extra pound or two. We were all string bean thin. Which reminds me of "*Stretch,*" "*Slim*" and "*the Pencil.*" Oh, by the way, *F.S.W.*'s Vietnamese name was Ong Anh. Translation: *Mr.*

*English*, in honor of Wally's heritage.

Today an expert in the contributions of Poles to American history, *"The Polack,"* formerly known as *"Alphabet"* because of the hodgepodge of consonants in his name boasted with pride that Polish jokes only served to spotlight his heritage. Likewise, it has become a common practice among some Black Americans today to adopt African names to solidly identify them with their ancestral roots.

I knew two Marines from the South Seas who were nicknamed *Pineapple*. One, a radio operator and native Hawaiian was a bantam weight boxer. He couldn't have weighed in at more than a 120 pounds.

The other, a "lifer" squad leader, was a monster Samoan who resembled a Sumo wrestler. A classic warrior, even in Vietnam he wore his sarong in the bush. Daily he would practice his machete juggling war dance to a tempo beat out on empty ammo cans. It was exhilarating to watch. Both had big, toothy grins, particularly when recognized for their heritage by the use of their nicknames.

The point is though, that not only as a nation, but also as distinct groups and individuals, we have lost our ability to interactively celebrate our ethnic pride and diversity.

I'm a war orphan. As a small child my elderly, maternal Grandparents played a significant role in my upbringing. Both were first generation Americans, born of Ellis Island immigrants. My grandfather was the son of German Jews, my Grandmother was Norwegian. I was raised Protestant, but because my paternal family was Catholic, I attended Parochial school. I have Asian and African-American godchildren. I've lived and worked all over the world, mostly with the indigenous population. Often times you would have had to travel for miles to see a white face other than mine. Sometimes I was ignored. Mostly I was embraced. I was always comfortable. Because I marvel at cultural differences, I have been called many names. I wear each with pride. That pride makes me bulletproof.

Four years ago I the recipient of slurs questioning my gender preference that were vile enough to boil the blood of most. The intent was to lure me into a physical confrontation by one who possessed the physical prowess to dismember me. For a brief second, I considered teaching him a lesson in humility. Instead, I volleyed his remarks with the look of compassion that one would give an idiot. His remarks only ceased for a moment, but in his eyes it was evident that he'd lost. He appeared to be just another loud-mouthed boob. Having a non-belligerent but proud posture won the day.

Any true citizen of the world will tell you that in the United States, in spite of our self-induced victim mentality, we don't have a clue what true discrimination is all about. The prejudice that we see between the Arabs and the Israelis, both Semitic peoples, is sometimes virulent. Ethnic bigotry is also found among Asians, Africans, Latinos and Europeans. We naively lump "them" all together because of similarities of color or physical features, but tribal intolerance on their own soil, makes America look like the Garden of Eden.

Network marketing, like the U.S., is a great and wonderful melting pot where each individual is recognized on his or her own merit. By being sensitive to individuals and groups when it comes to names, but unwilling to throw out our identity for the sake of knee-jerk political correctness, we proudly serve as an example for the rest of the world.

# 24

# Stuff or Freedom

*The Choice is Yours*

**Who has two Italian sports cars, a German Luxury Sedan**, a top of the line SUV, lives in a palace that looks like the Taj Mahal, wears six pounds of 18 caret gold studded with diamonds and has no furniture, 14 cents or less in their bank account and zero liquidity? Answer: a network marketing millionaire!

Obviously not true in all cases, but I never realized how pervasive and insidious this rock star mentality was when first introduced to network marketing over ten years ago. The leaders of that first organization earned millions but displayed an almost frugal lifestyle comparatively speaking. They exercised fiscal responsibility. Subsequent experience indicates that common sense about money is not the norm in this industry. Worse yet, it duplicates downline. In spite of outrageous earnings, many successful distributors are more encumbered with debt today than when they came into the industry.

A major revelation came several years ago when a national publication did a story on my success in networking. My primary residence at the time was a 170 year old historic mansion on a four and a half acre estate. It was a nice place but paled to the magnificent palaces in other such stories of achievement. I asked the photography crew why my home was selected when others were so much more splendid.

"How much do you owe on it?" was the reply.

"Nothing".

"Do you own your furniture?"

"Of course!"

"Most of the shoots we do involve folks who have enjoyed financial success such as yourself but are mortgaged so tightly that they have to rent furniture for the photo shoot! You are very unusual, my friend."

We see it time and again throughout the industry. The lure of big money, glitz and lifestyle so overwhelm many distributors that once they reach even a modicum of success, they feel it necessary to flash wealth to establish credibility. Nothing could be farther from the truth. Wealth, like poverty, is a state of mind, not a bank balance or a garage full of cars.

What many successful networkers don't understand is that the "flashy millionaire" glamorized by the media actually represents only a tiny minority of America's rich. Some of the wealthiest people in the country, folks worth eight figures and more, display little outward appearance of their affluence.

You might ask, "How can I get anybody 'in' if I can't show them a big check?" Your check bears no relevance to what your prospect may or may not earn. A check, like an expensive car or a thousand dollar suit, is only an issue if you make it one. When folks question your earnings, it's an indicator that your posture may be weak. Only twice in ten years has anyone asked me what I earned. Neither time did I answer them. Until three years ago I was driving a 1978 automobile. None of my suits cost more than $300. My next car was used. It was my attitude, not flash, that built my business.

If you go from making $35,000 a year to $135,000 a year or $1,035,000 a year and you trade your Ford for a Rolls Royce or your two bedroom rental for a Manhattan Penthouse, unless you pay cash, you are trading a little bit of debt for a lot of debt. Quite simply, you are broke at a higher level and still an indentured servant. You still have a financial ball and chain around your leg. Network marketing has done nothing for you but give you more junk to worry about. Cut that chain! Become debt-free. Learn what real wealth is all about: Freedom from financial worry. Peace of mind!

Forget what the personal development people say about rewarding yourself when you hit certain milestones. Forget instant gratification. Get out of debt first! Don't be like those unfortunate distributors who lost everything when their company took an unexpected mortal blow from government regulators or mismanagement by their own corporate big wigs.

Learn to live below your means. Sock something away for a rainy day. Learn the difference between an asset and a liability. Spend your money on appreciating or income-producing assets rather expense-producing liabilities.

Learn that you make your money when you buy, not when you sell.

You have the power of choice over every dollar that you spend or invest. Use that power wisely.

A few years back I was diagnosed with end stage heart disease. The odds didn't look good. The one saving grace was that I was debt free and wouldn't leave my family encumbered financially. I can't begin to tell you the comfort that simple fact offered me in those dark days.

Think about it!

# 25

# Mental Nutrition

*Feed your mind and you're on your way to earning millions!*

**Sixty per cent of Americans are overweight**, 8 million 100 pounds or more. More than half are obese. This means one third of all Americans are 20% or more heavier than their suggested body weight. That's usually a plus 30 pounds or more for a woman and a plus 50 pounds for a man. With elementary school kids, the statistics are even more alarming.

These numbers have exploded as fast food joints have proliferated. We've developed the habit of gorging ourselves with junk food. To that we add smoking and lack of exercise. There's no doubt we're killing ourselves. Where is our nutritional consciousness?

Mentally, we're not any better off. We feed our minds with junk. We sit in front of the tube and watch sitcoms that are so stupid we wouldn't know they were funny if they didn't have a laugh track. We addict ourselves to dysfunctional soap opera characters. We focus on the misery in our daily lives. We applaud the media for their pervasive proliferation of victimology. After all, we are victims. As a society, we adulate the political soothsayers of doom and gloom. We buy into their demagoguery. We feel good knowing that we are downtrodden. We feed our minds with negativity. There's no doubt that we're killing our spirit.

If you want to be successful in network marketing, or any endeavor, it's time to wake up. It's time to become both physically and mentally nutritionally conscious.

Eat well, fresh fruits and vegetables. Cut out the junk food. Exercise a little, even if it's just going for a daily walk. What physical well-being will do for your mental health is immeasurable, but you can create total sense of well-being by also consciously feeding your mind. It starts by avoiding mental junk food.

Develop the habit of associating with positive people. No one quits this industry who associates exclusively with positive people. There is an axiom that says that your life represents the average of the ten people with whom you most associate. Think about it! Where are your top ten associates financially? Emotionally? Physically? Are they comfortable? Are they cheerful? Are they successful? How about you? Are you where you want to be? If so, great! If not, you need to change your associations. If you're unwilling to do that, you're happy where you are.

Start by eliminating all of the negative influence in your life. It may be the TV. It may be the newspaper. It may be your friends. It may even be your spouse! Stop swimming tied to an anchor. Live your life with joy and excitement. Feel good about yourself!

Develop the habit of listening to motivational tapes for 30 minutes everyday. You could do this while going for a 30 minute walk and kill two birds with one stone. Invest 20 minutes everyday by reading. It'll exercise your mind and get your mental juices flowing. It'll give you a sense of euphoria.

I developed these habits years ago and have maintained them. Even though I have been incapacitated by heart disease and unable to pursue my network marketing business with the vigor that I once had, I still do these things. It's like spring training for the day when I'll be back on the playing field.

Stand up straight. Walk with a purpose. Always wear a smile on your face. These things will mentally nourish you. Coupled with a little physical exercise, you will be transformed into a super-being. You'll develop a sense of invincibility, which will put millions in your pocket. Why? Because success oriented folks like to associate with positive, self-confident people. The more positive you are, the more successful you'll be. There ain't many positive folks around, so you've got a leg up already.

By doing these things, you've established yourself as an example. People will want to be like you. The next step is to accelerate the process. Share your program with your organization. Provide them with suggestions for books and tapes. Go one step farther; provide them with some of the stuff that helped you.

Maybe you're not making any money yet? Maybe you feel that you can't afford to do this. Maybe you question whether or not it's duplicatable? So what? You're in business. Look at this as an investment that can return big dividends. Set this process in motion in your organization and it will duplicate.

What kind of stuff do you want to pass along? I believe that you need a potpourri of stuff: from inspirational, to validation of the industry, to a few techniques—anything that will help you to grow.

First I start with the staples. I have given away, by the case, nearly everything listed below: John Fogg's, *The Greatest Networker in the World*. It's become the de facto bible for the industry. In his new *Get Rich Slow*, John has encapsulated decades, probably centuries, of the perspectives of some of the great success gurus of all times. It's a must read, particularly for those students of success who appreciate reinforcement of already established success beliefs. John has ghost written a number of industry standards that have collectively sold over 3,000,000 copies. All of John Kalench's stuff is good, particularly *17 Secrets of Master Prospectors*.

Richard Brooke's *Mach II With Your Hair on Fire* explains vision, the most critical element, I'm convinced, to achieving success. His short book *Rags to Riches* provides inspirational stories of those who have made it. Also, *Breadwinner, Bread Baker,* Sandy Elsberg's semi-biographical sketch provides a great view of the industry from a woman's perspective, but it's a good read for every network marketer. Peggy Long's *On This Rock* may be the most all-encompassing book available on network marketing. It's the nuts and bolts manual. Robert Kiyosaki's books, *Rich Dad, Poor Dad* and *Cashflow Quadrant* remind us that earning the money is only half of the game.

*Wave3* and *Wave 4* by Richard Poe, *The New Professionals* by Dr Charles King, a Harvard economist and Rene Reid Yarnell's *The New Entrepreneurs*, all offer a tremendous overview of the industry and validate that we're in the right place at the right time.

*True Leadership* by Jan Ruhe and Art Burleigh, *The Joyful Spirit* by Brian Biro and *If How To's Were Enough* or the audiocassette series *Pursuit and Practice of Personal Mastery* by Brian Klemmer cause us to evaluate our own perspectives. I greatly enjoyed Brian's *Interviews with the Experts.*

A great video prospecting tape, which I also look at as a teaching tool for the neophyte, is *Brilliant Compensation* by Tim Sales.

I would also recommend anything by Tom Hopkins or Hilton Johnson. Hilton, I believe, is the best trainer in the sales industry today. His short, concise book, *The Hilton Johnson Collection*, cuts through all the fluff and lays out, in list form, the Top Ten steps for prospecting, presenting and marketing. Hilton has developed a life-coaching program that causes the student to seek the answers from within himself. Excellent stuff!

Some of the old standbys are, of course, *Think and Grow Rich* by Napoleon Hill and anything, book or cassette by Jim Rohn, Anthony Robbins, Brian Tracey, Denis Waitley, Mark Victor Hansen or Jack Canfield.

You can get most of these materials through Upline Publications. Some are available in bookstores or through Nightingale Conant.

Well, there you have it. You wouldn't go a day without nourishing your body, why would you go a day without feeding your mind? Well nourished or malnourished? The choice is yours!

# 26

# Enslavement or Freedom?

*The Choice is Yours!*

**A few weeks ago Gingie and I were invited by a former cabinet level official to attend a formal ceremony in Washington D.C.** honoring thirteen surviving members of a 45 man Marine Corps combat platoon. The next day we attended a small, private cookout at the Secretary's home. In attendance were the heroes and their wives, a couple of generals and a few nationally known political commentators.

Almost unnoticed on one corner of the deck, were several folks that I recognized as Vietnamese. I knew that they must enjoy some prominence to be invited to this exclusive affair. I asked my host who they were?

I'll just tell you about one.

At age 28 he was one of the youngest commanders in the Vietnamese Army. He had already received his country's Medal of Honor. After the fall of Saigon he was captured and sent North to be interred in a re-education camp. These camps are more than just political indoctrination classes. They are designed to break the human spirit by utilizing the two greatest psychological tortures known to humanity—-isolation and fear of the unknown.

Visualize his experience. Upon arrival, he was thrown in a box. A cage would have been more humane. The box, about the size of a large doghouse with a metal door, was actually a cistern for ground water.

He had no room to stand up or lay down. He was forced to sit in total darkness with his head bowed and his knees drawn up to his chest. He had no idea how long he would be confined in this manner. It could be hours. It could be days. Or it could be until his death! He didn't know if he'd ever get out.

His only contact, outside of his own mind, were the mosquitoes, and if you've never been in a tropical climate without insect repellent, you don't know what mosquitoes are, and the rats, which can weasel through even the tiniest of openings in their search for food. Both viewed him as a protein source.

He sat like this hour after hour after hour. When he had to relieve himself there was nowhere to go. He was condemned to wallow in his own filth.

The only way that he could tell the difference between day and night were periods of stifling, suffocating heat alternating with periods of damp, bone chilling cold, and always, always the incessant droning of mosquitoes buzzing in his ears.

The mosquito and rat bites quickly became infected. He developed dysentery and diarrhea. He competed for space with his own waste. He became emaciated. His teeth rotted out. The stench was overwhelming. He nearly went blind. Still he endured:   Hour after hour. Day after day. Week after week. Month after month. Year after year, for five and a half long years.

Can you imagine one hundredth of one per cent of what he endured? Imagine sitting naked for just an hour in your own closet being attacked by ravenous mosquitoes and starving rats.

When he was released from the box he was still kept in solitary confinement. His condition had deteriorated so badly that it took him years before he could stand or function on the most rudimentary level.

His wife, pregnant at the time of his incarceration, was finally allowed to visit him. She would travel over a thousand miles for one fifteen-minute visit a year. When he was released after twelve and a half years he met his thirteen-year-old son for the first time.

I asked him where he found the inner strength to survive.

In broken English, he humbly replied, "I dreamed of the United States. I dreamed of freedom for my family. If I died they would never escape. I had to live."

Ladies and Gentleman, you have a free ride.

As we journey through life we are constantly challenged by events that can break our spirit. Maybe we feel unappreciated. Maybe our feelings are hurt by those to whom we are most loyal. But just as this officer did a decade ago, we must focus on our will to live and our escape to freedom.

It may take 2 or 3 years, or even ten years to escape. But your challenges pale in comparison to those obstacles faced by my compatriot.

Use a few products and share them with others. Keep an eye open for those who are also looking for freedom. If you can't find the courage to address these small tasks, then you have chosen to spend the rest of your life in that box that you have created for yourself.

Enslavement or freedom? The choice is yours!

# Conclusion
# Coming in for a Landing

*We will be boarding soon for the next leg of the journey.*

**All passengers kindly return to your seats**. Place your seatbacks in their full upright and locked position and return your tray tables to the closed and locked position in the seatbacks in front of you. Fasten your seat belts and prepare for landing.

We have landed. All passengers may disembark. For those who wish to continue, the itinerary for the second phase of the journey is complete. Our upcoming destinations include: Loyalty, Relativity, Originality, Duplication, Tenacity, Fear, Self-discipline and Teamwork.

I invite you to continue. This journey is for you. I've been there. More than anything, I want you to become successful. I will relive my journeys and the lessons that I've learned whether you accompany me or not, but it's always more fun with a traveling companion.

Again, for maximum impact, I encourage you to go back and select one chapter at a time. Read and re-read that chapter, pausing each time to reflect on and embrace the message of that particular chapter. Then, pass that message along to others.

Thank you and God Bless!

## *Build a powerful organization of leaders*

Acclaimed by industry leaders as the definitive MANUAL for developing leaders and building people for long-term success.

*Reflections* will inspire your organization and focus their thoughts and energy. It has the principles, speaks to the heart and stirs one to action!

You can place orders for yourself and your organization over the Internet through the following websites:

    networkingtimes.net

or visit www.frankkeefer.com for additional sources of distribution and generous volume discounts.

Frank may be contacted at fjk@frankkeefer.com

All profits from the sale of this book will be donated to charity.

If you enjoyed **Reflections**, standby for the concluding volume in this series:

# Continuing the Journey

*Excerpts*:

•"Like a huge, voracious monster, the 5000 foot black and gray vertical wall abruptly appeared out of nowhere. It chased our small plane across the landscape. Suddenly, it was upon us! The massive thunderstorm, in one ravenous gulp, swallowed us whole. Inside its belly, we were violently battered and tossed about like a piece of trash in a tropical hurricane. There was no doubt in our minds, we were dead!"

•"Thirty-five years ago the majority of shows were still in black and white. But, the dream of every American family was a color TV. By pinching pennies, my wife and I purchased one. A proud accomplishment for a $7,000 a year school teacher living in a tiny apartment."

•"The whistle blew. The world around me disappeared. Like a laser beam, my mind focused totally on destroying my opponent. At breakneck speed we charged each other, swinging maniacally. There would be no draw. I would either win or lose. Survival was the name of the game!"

•Retired Master Sergeant James R. Whitlock was one of the finest soldiers I have ever known. This veteran of WWII and the Korean War and I had made a couple of skydives together a dozen years earlier. I hadn't spoken to him since that time.

"Hey Top*, Frank Keefer."

"Captain! How ya doin, Sir?"

"Magnificent! How'd ya like to make a parachute jump?"

"Great!"

"It's an equipment jump."

"I'm in!"

In little more than a dozen words, this man committed to trusting me with his life. The only equipment jumps are military, not skydives. Both of us were civilians. Why would we jump military gear? He didn't ask.

*Dignity, Pride, Tenacity* and *Leadership* are just a few of the stops we will make in the concluding volume in this series.

* "Top" - a term of respect for Master Sergeants

# Other Books by the Author

*Let's Get Down to Business*

# About the Author

Frank Keefer is co-founder of *Network Marketing Lifestyles Magazine*. Under his direction as President and Chief Executive Officer, the magazine became the number one start-up publication in 1999 and the number one business publication on the newsstands that year. By the end of year one, the magazine was in 22 countries.

He has over twelve years in the network marketing industry and achieved the top pin level in three companies. Frank is known for his no nonsense approach to business. He has probably created more high-dollar earners per capita in a shorter period of time than anyone in the history of the industry.

Prior to network marketing, he was a highly successful executive in the pharmaceutical, advertising and high tech industries serving with such Fortune Fifty corporations as Revlon, Johnson & Johnson, Philips of North America and Motorola. He was the owner or a principle in a half dozen diverse businesses including sports aviation and international security.

An Honor graduate of the University of Baltimore, he completed 4 years in two years and was elected to the Honor Society. He taught high school and was a single parent for ten years.

Frank honed his leadership skills in the U.S. Marine Corps and the U.S. Army Special Forces (Green Berets) and Rangers. He was one of only a very few to receive a Direct Commission as an infantry officer for combat leadership in Vietnam where he was wounded in action.

He was a world-class parchutist, a high-ranking black belt in the martial arts, as well as a mountain climbing and scuba instructor.

Over the past four decades his adventures have been prominently featured numerous times in the national media.

He currently lives with the love of his life, Gingie, on the Wye River in Maryland. His home was the site of the 1998 Mid East Peace Accords.

He has three grown children, Lucille, Richard and Frank III, who has followed him into the industry.